WPRI N

CRITICAL PERSPECTIVES
ON EMPOWERMENT

Editor
Beth Humphries

Published by
VENTURE PRESS
16 Kent Street
Birmingham
B5 6RD

British Library Cataloguing-in-Publication Data
A catalogue record for this book is available from the British Library

ISBN 1 873878 50 8 (paperback)

Cover design by
Western Arts
194 Goswell Road,
London ECIV 7DT

Printed in Great Britain

Preface

The motivations for this book have been several, though first amongst them is a concern at the plethora of books and articles on *empowerment* which have emerged over the past 10 years or so. These have largely represented *empowerment* in reductionist and simplistic ways, implying that *empowerment* is simply a matter of will, either on the part of those who are disempowered, or on the part of those in a position to *empower* In this literature there is an absence of any context for discussions of *empowerment* or any questions as to why *empowerment* is a concept claimed by advocates right and left of the political spectrum, or as to its popularity at this historical moment. What is on offer is a range of prescriptions for *empowerment,* cookbooks for how to achieve it. Moreover there is in the literature no real attempt to theorise the notion of *empowerment* or to explore the social effects achieved by its use. Underpinning the discussions is an assumption that empowerment is a "good thing" both for those without power and for professionals as part of their practice.

The book is an attempt to go beyond these recipes, indeed not to offer recipes at all, rather to foreground the notion as a complex and multifaceted phenomenon which has regulatory as well as emancipatory potential. The chapters taken together offer perspectives on the political, social and educational context in which empowerment discourses take place (Gillman; Green, Martin and Williams); they ask questions as to who sets the agenda for empowerment, who defines the problem and what frameworks of knowledge are used (Anderson); they explore the potential of contemporary theories to offer a framework for making sense of empowerment (Price; Fawcett and Featherstone; Carabine); they examine the disciplinary power of professional socialisation (Gillman) and the conflict between liberatory struggle and institutional agendas (Green, Martin and Williams; they consider the possibilities for activism across different issues (Lynn and Muir); they uncover the contradictory nature of empowerment (Humphries); and they expose the ways in which those who "speak for" those without power, reinforce rather than challenge powerlessness (Novak). All of the chapters search for ways of understanding empowerment which refuse to reduce it to simplistic concepts or sloganising jargon, and which politicise the notion in ways which are absent from other discussions.

Represented in this volume are a range of perspectives which reflect ongoing debates in the wider society. The topics and ideas are contested, and the authors would take issue with each other on fundamental understandings. This is no bad thing, for it allows dialogue and exchange of views towards a more informed use of current concepts. At the heart of all the essays, however, is a scepticism of common-sense notions of empowerment, a systemic view of power needing to be examined and a sense of people *coming to their own empowerment through individual and collective action.*

The book is entitled Critical Perspectives on Empowerment. The word *critical* has become as fashionable as empowerment and is also used in all sorts of different ways: therefore it needs some explanation here. Like empowerment, assumptions are made that to be "critical" is desirable (who would want to be seen as *un*critical?), and they are employed to describe particular approaches in disciplines across the social sciences and within the humanities. Hammersley offers a wide-ranging discussion on the problems which result from claims to be 'critical' in approaches derived from both modernist and postmodernist traditions. In a critique he argues that it does not represent a single, coherent approach and that, as a label, "critical" has lost any cognitive value it may have had: it is an empty rhetorical shell. Its use amounts to an attempt to disguise a particular set of substantive and political commitments as a universal position that gives epistemological and moral privilege (Hammersley 1995:43)

This is a rather polemical conclusion, not justified by Hammersley's preceding discussion. Patti Lather (1991) takes a different position, arguing the possibilities for a critical social science in asking questions of power, economy, history and exploitation. She sees the various feminisms, neo-Marxisms and some of the poststructuralists as critical theories informed by identification with and interest in oppositional social movements. In her view the central questions of critical Inquiry are: How do our very efforts to liberate perpetuate dominance? (page 16) and: What would a sociological project look like that was not a technology of regulation and surveillance? (page 15). In her discussion of critical social research Lather proposes a praxis-oriented paradigm, that is, "that we who do empirical research in the name of emancipatory politics must discover ways to connect our research methodology to our theoretical concerns and political commitments" (Lather 1991:172). The various authors in this collection may use interpretations which can be seen as conflicting, but a distinctive feature of the debates posited here as *critical* is a commitment to political goals - to show connections which are hidden, to provide resources for those disadvantaged through change, to understand the world *and* to change it.

I am indebted to each of the contributors who willingly agreed to write a chapter on this important subject in the midst of other demands and pressures, and who made every effort to meet the deadlines. I wish also to record thanks to Malcolm Payne, the general editor of the series *Advocacy and Empowerment,* for his encouragement and support.

References

Hammersley, M. (1995) *The Politics of Social Research* Sage

Lather, P. (1991) Getting Smart: *Feminist research and pedagogy with/in the post-modern* Routledge

Contents

The Authors

Jill Anderson currently divides her time among paid and unpaid work ranging from teaching in adult and higher education on health and women's issues, to running health sessions with small local groups, to running a women's health drop-in and running around after her two-year-old son. Her chequered past includes time in medical research, teaching in Kenya, and voluntary work in Hulme, Manchester. She has participated in three rapid appraisal projects to ascertain local needs.

Jean Carabine, lecturer in social policy, Department of Social Science, University of Loughborough, is author of *Women, Sexuality and Social Policy,* Macmillan (forthcoming), and recent articles on politics, sexuality and social policy. She is a member of the editorial collective of the journal *Critical Social Policy*

Barbara Fawcett BSc, MSc, CQSW has worked in a variety of social work settings for the past 12 years as a practitioner, manager and systems researcher. Her experience includes working with homeless families, children and families, disabled people and people experiencing mental distress. Currently she is carrying out research into meanings attached to disability and the implications of perspectives drawn from feminist post-modernist and post-structural writings. She lecturers currently in social work at the University of Bradford. She has published articles on community care, mental health, social work theory and practice and disability.

Brid Featherstone studied sociology at Trinity College Dublin 1974 to 1978. She qualified as a social worker in 1982. She worked with young women offenders and in the field of child protection as a social worker and team manager. She has undertaken research into alternatives to custody and is currently research-ing for a PhD on the subject of women's violence to children. She co-edited with Barbara Fawcett, Jeff Hearn and Chris Toft *Violence and Gender Relations: Theories and Interventions* (forthcoming from Sage). She is currently co-editing with Wendy Holloway a book entitled Mothering and Ambivalence, which will be published by Routledge in 1996.

Dr Maureen Gillman qualified as a social worker in 1976 and worked for Newcastle upon Tyne Social Services Department for 10 years. In 1986 she was employed as a research assistant at the University of Northumbria at Newcastle and was awarded a PhD in 1994. She currently works for the university as a senior lecturer and has research interests in the fields of disability and systemic practice.

Mary Green is co Co-ordinator of Education for Primary Health Care courses and co Co-ordinator of Gender and Education for the Primary Health Care course, University of Manchester. Her previous work experience has been as a community health worker and health promotion officer in inner city areas in the UK. She spent two years in Sierra Leone as a trainer and co-ordinator of a traditional midwife programme, and four and a half years in Swaziland in the field of public health, health promotion and training. Mary's research interests include inequity in health with a specific interest in gender and primary health care. Currently she is researching into how these areas are incorporated into mainstream health training with appropriate methodology.

Beth Humphries has worked, taught and researched in social work for a number of years. She was awarded her PhD by the University of Edinburgh in 1983. Her present job is director of postgraduate studies in the Department of Applied Community Studies at the Manchester Metropolitan University. She is author of *Understanding Research* and co-editor (with Carole Truman) of *Rethinking Social Research.*

Elisabeth Lynn is a white Welsh woman. She works as a part-time lecturer on the social work course at the University of Wales, Bangor and is researching the implementation of anti-oppressive practice within the Diploma in Social Work. Although experiencing oppression, she is watchful of her oppressor side and believes in the need to scrutinise notions of empowerment; it is only by grasping this complex nettle that a way forward can be found. The current position of social work education and the Welsh language in Wales offers a fresh approach to long-standing dilemmas.

Marion Martin has worked and researched in community health and education and has publications in participatory and feminist research, adult learning and professional education. She is co-editor (with Korrie de Koning) of *Participatory Research In Health: Issues and Experiences.* She has worked in the UK and south India and has research experience in Tanzania. Marion is co-ordinator of the diploma/masters course in Education for Primary Health Care and the Gender Education and PHC course at the Centre for Adult and Higher Education, University of Manchester.

Allan Muir is a white, middle class English male whose experience is of the oppressor's side of most major social divisions. His concern with oppression stems from his working class background and his political grounding is Marxist; another source is his Catholic upbringing, which created a feeling of exclusion from English society, but also a revulsion against power and dogma. He adopts a rationlist, sceptical approach deriving from the Enlightenment (*pace* postmodernists), an attitude confirmed by a life in theoretical natural science. He is now engaging with a previously unconsidered oppression through coming to live in Wales.

Tony Novak has written about, researched and been active in community politics around poverty for the past 20 years. He currently lectures in social policy in the Department of Sociology, Social Policy and Social Work Studies, University of Liverpool.

Janet Price is affiliated to the University of Liverpool though unemployed due to ill health. She teaches on feminist health issues, and her recent experience of illness and disability led her to become increasingly involved in addressing where and how bodies fit into feminist theorising and practice. She has been developing the art of gardening for small spaces in her terrace backyard, and is learning to do textiles and embroidery work without neatening all the edges.

Jan Williams is lecturer in Health Promotion at the Faculty of Medicine at the University of Manchester. She has a background in health services research, health promotion and organisation and management development. Her current teaching interests relate principally to postgraduate education of professionals in public health and health promotion. She is committed to promoting a more holistic view of education and the use of student-centred approaches in the academic environment.

Chapter 1
Contradictions in the Culture of Empowerment

Beth Humphries

Introduction

We are living in a period of profound contradiction. The rhetoric of empowerment drops on our heads at every turn like confetti, its mention directly or by implication *de rigueur* in articles, books and political statements. It has become a key objective in the training of professionals of all kinds, particularly in the 'caring' professions. At the same time we are witnessing an historic *shift* of power on a global scale (Townsend 1993). In Britain most young middle class people, as well as manual workers, now realise they cannot expect lifetime employment. The banks, insurance companies, government bureaucracies, are all laying off staff to swell the ranks of the 'anxious class'. Fascism is on the rise, feeding as it always does on the despair of the middle class. Many of the big companies who offered permanent employment and security have halved their workforce and some of the biggest have disappeared altogether (Sampson 1995). Companies now feel no political pressure to provide welfare, unions have been rapidly weakened by new technological industries, privatisation and unemployment. Both managers and workers are helpless to resist the layoffs. Whilst the 'company man' has seen a decline in his security, the bosses have enjoyed a freedom and a dominating position not known since the beginning of the century. The publicity around what have been called 'astonishing' and 'obscene' (Observer June 4,1995) payments to corporate chiefs has also revealed the powerlessness of shareholders to curtail this obscenity.

Meanwhile, at the other end of the social scale, the character of poverty and disadvantage accelerates and deepens with the approach of the year 2000. Britain is a more unequal society than at any time since the 1930s (JRF Inquiry Group 1995), and the gap between rich and poor nations increases daily (Novak, this volume). The concept of the underclass is a central feature of attempts to criminalise the poor as a way of legitimating this inequality (Murray 1990). Thus the trend has been towards *social exclusion, polarisation* and *marginalisation*, not towards inclusion and 'empowerment'.

There have been substantial increases in the rate of psychosocial disorders, particularly in young people across Europe and North America (Rutter and Smith 1995). These include suicidal behaviour, depression, eating abnormalities, drugs and alcohol misuse. The rate of suicide has sharply increased, especially in young males, whilst evidence of depression is twice as high in young women as young men. Health and mortality statistics show a deterioration in health worldwide, and a return of diseases associated with poverty. Doyal (1995) describes growing inequalities in women's mortality rates across social groups globally, and Craig and Mayo (1995) identify major differences between rich and poor nations.

This reality reveals contradiction in the culture of empowerment which has enveloped us, contradictions which can be observed at a number of levels, and needs some exploration. It is the purpose of this chapter to attempt to examine the significance of the rise of a discourse of 'empowerment', identifying contradiction as a central theme. Contradiction is an inherent part of contemporary human experience often not acknowledged in the literature which typically strives to *iron out* wrinkles in people's experiences rather than *describe* and seek explanations for them. It is my objective here to acknowledge contradiction as an important theoretical construct, to explore contradictions surrounding the concept of *empowerment*, and to ask why a discourse of empowerment is so dominant in global society at this historical moment. Such an understanding will need also to take account particularly of the *context* in which claims to empowerment are made, and the way in which particular groups are *represented*.

I shall focus on two interconnected phenomena characteristic of the end of the twentieth century: bureaucratic equal opportunities policies and particular social movements based on identity politics.

Equal Opportunities Policies: A Tremendous Hopelessness
It may seem unduly pessimistic to give this section a title which is so negative in its expectations, but it embodies the contradictions I want to unpack. The push towards equal opportunities policies gathered momentum in both the UK and the USA in the 1970s and 1980s, to the point where employers and educational institutions would be ashamed not to declare themselves publicly as EO employers. Now, crumbling under legal challenge or under accusations of 'political correctness', in Britain they are quietly being dropped by local authorities and other employers. In the USA the backlash against affirmative action legislation (and feminism and 'multiculturalism') is not so quiet, and after some highly publicised challenges, some States are having to change the law and some universities are abandoning speech and behaviour codes. In the culture war that characterises contemporary life, the crusading spirit of the conservative agenda is most powerfully conveyed through its negative rhetoric: anti-social welfare, anti-intellectuals, anti-universities, anti-public funding for the arts and humanities, anti-minorities.

As Homi Bhabha (Guardian July 8, 1995) puts it, it is not clear what 'family values' stand *for* but they do stand *against* abortion rights, gay rights and all forms of affirmative action, 'a term that covers the great unwashed, migrants, minorities and the poor'. As I write, the University of California at Berkeley, traditionally in the vanguard of change, is considering abandoning what is seen as the essence of affirmative action - admission policies to increase numbers of black and minority ethnic students. The State Governor has issued an executive order sharply curtailing affirmative action in State government (reported in The Times Higher June 16, 1995). What California does today the rest of America does tomorrow.

The reasons for these changes are complex and multifaceted, and I intend only to focus on those aspects which are the focus of the chapter. The optimism underlining the trend towards EO concealed flaws both in the conception and in the implementation of EO which require examination. There are a number of strands in the contradiction.

Equality on unequal terms
First, EO policies were based on the liberal assumption that inequality equals discrimination. In other words, the society was at root sound, with discrimination against some groups a superficial blemish which could be manipulated away - a wart on the face of the good community. Ramazanoglu (1989) puts her finger on the problem when she says of EO policies:

> Societies dominated by racist ideologies and with discriminatory practices cannot meet the needs of subordinate races or ethnic groups for freedom from domination *while also meeting the needs of the dominating groups to dominate*. Societies which legitimate men's power over women cannot satisfy women's interest in freedom from men *and also men's interest in continued domination*. (p177, my italics).

Of course the issues are even more complex that this, since there are also contradictory interests amongst different ethnic groups and amongst women, and I return to this below. The point here is that EO represents an attempt to resolve the problems of domination within the forms of social organisation which gave rise to them. The widening gap between rich and poor and the decreasing opportunities for marginalised groups are testimony to the absence of a foundation based on a genuine attempt towards changing social structures.

Equality and hierarchies of oppression
In Britain the construction of EO policies in local government was based on a number of erroneous assumptions. The first was that the interests of widely

disparate groups, identified as 'Women', 'Black people', 'Gay', 'Lesbian', 'Disabled' are inherently non-conflicting and intrinsically the same, because they are all, in the words of Anthias and Yuval-Davis (1993) *categories of disadvantage:*

> having to be categorised as underprivileged and to become slotted into a
> hierarchy of rival disadvantage in order to complete equally in a climate of
> 'materialistic individualism', could be interpreted as a contradiction (p192).

In fact the only 'commonality' amongst these groups was disadvantage. The various groups viewed themselves in very different ways. Being forced to bid against each other for scarce resources resulted in bitterness and antagonism, arguments as to 'which are the most oppressed' and exacerbation of an unwillingness to search for a common cause. The essentialism of difference which arises from this reduced individuals to an all-encompassing and exclusive category. One aspect of such reductionism is a rejection of the complexity of lived experience, since many people could potentially belong to more than one category. Moreover, there is an assumption within such a construction of EO that the categories are internally homogeneous, accepting undemocratically chosen 'leaders' as representing all, and obscuring exclusions and conflicts of interest and power within them. Further, the policies assumed that all popular causes are necessarily progressive. As Anthias and Yuval-Davis (1993) write '. . . the categorising of people becomes a useful vehicle by which to grind individual axes which often perpetuates racism, homophobia, sexism, etc.' (p189). Amongst the competing demands, the fragmentation, the divisiveness, the notion of equal opportunities became largely meaningless, paving the way for an individualistic backlash exploited by Thatcherism and pursued in the 'political correctness' accusations of her successors (Dunant 1994).

One of the ways the British Right has capitalised on the competitiveness of different interests is by 'repackaging meanings' and by representing *difference* as alienation, as evidence that groups with different cultural origins and practices cannot live together successfully. The logical end of this argument is exclusion of 'the Other' through a tightening of immigration legislation, or introducing laws forbidding local authority support to groups such as gay men and lesbians. Government policy has been closely followed by New Labour in, for example, its abandonment of all-women shortlists of parliamentary candidates in certain constituencies (Observer, August 6, 1995).

Equality and self-interest
Emancipation pushes in the direction of both self-interest and ethics (ie the interests of others). Above I have argued that EO policies assumed a sympathy

amongst disadvantaged groups that did not in fact exist. Indeed an outright antagonism often existed which flourished in the culture of EO. An example of the push towards self-interest is the issue of cultural relativism - a conflict between the urge to respect different cultures and cultural practices whilst at the same time holding to a respect for dominated groups such as women and their rights. In a number of instances, respect for culture difference has dominated over respect for women, resulting in the justification of inhuman practices. Two competing sets of ethics have led to worrying trends based on assumptions about the liberatory nature of the popular movements referred to above. At times the Greater London Council (regarded as the most forward-looking local authority in the UK) was funding both repressive right wing groups on grounds of 'empowering communities' and 'multiculturalism', whilst at the same time supporting the efforts of black women to organise themselves against certain cultural practices. Sahgal (1992) argues that local Labour councils seldom questioned whether the funding they offered to other groups conflicted with their support for women's groups.

Yasmin Ali, (1992) in discussing the failure of anti-racism policies, suggests that, in a hostile political climate and amongst other problems in their conception, there was a lack of explicitness in their attempts to deliver the promise of a democratic route out of marginalisation for minority communities. The central contradiction was not confronted: 'the proper recognition of a need for black minority autonomy in the development of political strategies and organisation too easily became an excuse for not recognising or engaging with sexism in black organisations' (Ali 1992:116).

Setting the contradictions in context
The context of all this in Britain was the Thatcher government entering its second term of office in 1983 with local government clearly in its sights as needing radical reform. Equal opportunities policies were represented as wasting ratepayers' money, fostering divisions along racial lines, interfering with freedom, promoting left-wing ideas and undermining British culture (Gordon 1990). In Britain as in the USA over the past two years the backlash has raged unabated. Examples of mistakes made in the name of EO, accusations of 'political correctness (Humphries 1993, Dunant 1994)) have resulted in a dismantling of confidence in equal opportunity and left the EO and anti-racist lobbies dazed and defensive.

The emphasis of these attacks removes the spotlight from the very effective way in which the government of the day *itself* has commanded the ideological territory by confronting moral issues in education, sexuality and sexual behaviour and 'the family'. What was set in train was a powerful anti-welfare consensus which has impacted on the material reality of all our lives. The trick that was achieved was that the Right condemned as politically correct the gaps and shortcomings of EO, while at the same time aggressively setting the parameters of public debate. As Hall comments. . .

> . . . we are talking about the use of political power in order to 'wind up' one whole historical era - the welfare state, Keynesian, full-employment, comprehensive education era on which the post-war settlement was constructed and its replacement by another entirely new type of social order (Hall 1994:170).

This is the breadth of the context in which a discourse of empowerment flourishes. Bureaucratic EO policies have been replaced by, on the one hand, a culture of 'pulling yourself up by the bootstraps' and, on the other, a sense of desperation that if you don't do it nobody else will. The professional language of 'empowering others' (see for example Ward and Mullender 1992) implies an acceptance of this redefinition away from gender, 'race' and class exploitation and the introduction of a modern version of individualistic casework models with 'empowerment' as the goal, but without substance or political power.

EO policies and legislation have not been entirely without success in opening up opportunities to disadvantaged groups, or at least to particular individuals within these groups. Moreover, while they have not sought to change fundamental inequalities, but rather to seek equality on the terms already set by dominant social groups, they have exposed the monopoly of power by privileged groups, largely white middle class men, and thus have helped politicise their power and (perhaps) to make them more accountable. *Nevertheless the underpinning assumption brings us back to where we started, with a period of searching for equality without dismantling unequal structures, followed by the fallacy of increased 'choice' without engaging political power.* In a different context Nancy Fraser argues that affirmative action programmes, since they do not aim for a transformation of structures, leave intact the deep structures that generate disadvantage. They result in marking the most disadvantaged as always needing more and more, as inherently deficient and insatiable: 'In time such a class can even come to appear privileged, the recipient of special treatment and undeserved largesse' (Fraser 1995:85).

Social movements – oppositional and reactionary forces
A key feature in the collapse of equal opportunities policies was the emergence of identity politics, which challenged the assumptions that allowed groupings to

suspend the differences among them in the struggle for equality. In this section I explore complexities in the notion of empowerment, based on an examination of contemporary phenomena linked to particular social movements which claim empowerment for their members. Such claims are puzzling if one regards them solely as reassertions of 'difference' or oppositional agency, since the movements with which they are associated are often manifestly sexist and/or racist, and sometimes Fascist. What then are we to make of these claims? I argue that subjective feelings should not be the only criterion upon which to evaluate claims to empowerment, and that the themes of contradiction, context and representation should be fundamental to any attempt to understand both the discursive and material realities inherent in these assertions of empowerment. I shall be drawing on a framework I have developed elsewhere, Humphries (1994) for the purpose of interrogating claims to empowerment.

Effective gendering: constructing constriction as choice
Spivak (1991) uses this term in an attempt to explain the position of those women caught within the politics of paternalism and dedicated to the furtherance of patriarchal groups which offer them responsibility without power. Such women often occupy key roles and responsibility for keeping an organisation or a movement going, but are restricted in the range of roles and the access to power they may have. By way of explaining their situation they and others describe their position as taken by choice, whereas their choices are indeed constricted and other possibilities are not open to them.

Campbell (1987) has written in these terms about Conservative women. Maitland (1992) describes how in the neo-evangelical Christian movement in the ascendant in the USA and Britain, despite a rhetoric of 'freedom' and 'deliverance', it is largely authoritarian, reactionary and censorious. Yuval-Davis (1992) shows how women in some Jewish fundamentalist groups are represented as a source of special strength, knowledge and power. But such autonomy as they have is constructed within *male-defined women's space*. Deviants who do not adhere to the very strict rules of internal authority and closed ranks are dealt with harshly. Sahgal and Yuval-Davis (1992) identify the central paradox for women in fundamentalist groups:

> . . . the fact that women collude, seek comfort, and even at times gain a
> sense of empowerment within the spaces allocated to them. . . . It can
> be . . . a space for personal accomplishment to which unskilled working-
> class women and frustrated middle-class women might be attracted.

For women of racial and ethnic minorities, it can also provide the means by
which to defend themselves as well as to defy the hegemonic racist culture.
. . . However, the overall effect of fundamentalist movements has been very
detrimental to women, limiting and defining their roles and activities and
actively oppressing them. . . (p9).

Mazumdar (1995) identifies a similar dynamic for women in the Hindu fundamentalist movement and I now want to look at their assertions as a way of
addressing the general issues arising from the phenomenon of fundamentalism.
Mazumdar asks the question: What are the ways in which gender ideology is
recast and manipulated to aid the growth of this political movement?

Over the past decade the rise of Hindu Fascism in India has resulted in the death of
thousands of Muslims and widespread destruction. Throughout the riots, women
have played a highly visible role, leading mobs dragging Muslim women and
children into the streets, applauding their gang rapes. These are not women
awaiting protection and rescue but women who symbolise the qualities necessary
for the 'ideal' Indian woman, Strength, Intellect and Wealth.

Like the Nazi women who risked arrest, were courageous and spirited in
supporting Nazi activities and rejected the stereotype of the meek and
submissive woman, the RSS-BJP-VHP women too are on the move
Mazumdar (1995:18).

A sense of self-confidence for these Hindu women comes with their role as
warriors, declaring themselves to be 'sparks of fire' as they dedicate themselves to
struggle on the front line.

In order to understand this situation a number of points need to be made. We
should consider the context in which activism takes place and the contradictions
inherent in the experience of these women. First, their position as front-line
fighters appears to give them confidence and assertiveness, but if an analysis of
empowerment is grounded in the struggle for survival of the most disadvantaged
and the poorest, not in the privileging of a particular group as the norm or referent
(Humphries 1994), these are not disadvantaged women. The movement to which
they belong is supported by the middle classes and the *petit bourgeois*. The
women form the remnant of a feudal aristocracy and indeed are likely to gain their
confidence as much from their being a hegemonic class and their wealth than from
their role as warriors. According to Mazumdar the Indian Government has
encouraged the privileging of Hindu culture and given it a certain patriotic legiti-
macy (although see Sahgal 1992 for a more complex picture). Parties associated

with Hindu fundamentalism now control a number of key Indian states and cities. We are not here talking about an oppressed group rising up against their oppression. The most disadvantaged and the poorest are those women, men and children who have been constructed as alien and as traitors, and have become the victims of an oppressive regime.

A second contradiction relates to constriction of choices for these warrior women. The power they exercise is in respect of (i) the cultural sphere in educating children in traditional values, and as teachers to carry the word to secluded women, and (ii) the slaughter of women and children of minorities seen to be inferior and obstructive to building the Hindu nation. But men still hold the most powerful leadership positions. Mazumdar argues that this seeming support for a public role for women does not mean a transformation of patriarchal relations in the long term.

> ... patriarchy remains sacrosanct; the ideal woman is one who has 'intellectual grasp of the values of Hindu culture and devotional attachment to the ideals of Hindu womanhood' (Mazumdar 1995: 20)

Women's domestic role is reaffirmed both in official rhetoric and by the women themselves, and there is no relief from their duties as wives and mothers. Indeed there is a question over whether married women should be involved as activists, with contradictions between supporting motherhood and family while drawing on the energies of youthful volunteers. The movement's vision of an appropriate role for women is apparent in a decline in the literacy rate for women in States where Hindu nationalists have gained control; the slashing of reserved teaching quotas for women from 50% to 3%; the encouragement to families to increase the numbers of children as protection against supposedly proliferating Muslim hoardes. This reveals a situation of *exploitation*, and shows the ways in which 'constriction is constructed as choice'. Moreover, not all Hindu women have given their assent to these conditions. Sahgal (1992) reports that some women have had their behaviour forcibly changed and that the opposition of feminists means that the practices do not go uncontested. Hindu women are not an homogeneous group.

The position of Hindu fundamentalist women illustrates the multiple, fluid structures of power, *exercised* rather than *possessed*, as identified by Foucault (1980) and included in my framework referred to above. It reveals a back and forward movement of power, with both structural dominance and structural subordination in play in complex, multifaceted power relations. It is particularly important to note the fluidity of these women's identities, moving from a role as warrior women to one of domestic responsibility as wives and mothers. To speak of empowerment or oppression in reductionist and static ways is not helpful, since contradiction is an inherent characteristic of experience. However, in terms of *representation*, the case of Hindu fundamentalist women is instructive. The view of these women as 'warriors' cuts across stereotypes of Asian women as passive and compliant. At the same time they clearly are not 'feminine' in any conventional sense, since women are not expected to encourage and take part in murder and rape. This results in a confirmation of pathologising views of Asian women *whichever* way they are represented.

In fact, in terms of gender relations, the case study I have offered here is a particular and perhaps extreme example of a much more universal phenomenon. Lest it is used to feed into racist stereotypes, the contextualising of the case example needs to be widened even further than its cultural and geographical boundaries. Yuval-Davis, in discussing differences in gender relations within different ethnic and national groupings, identifies one characteristic which specifies women's citizenship:

> That is its dualistic nature – on the one hand women are always included, at least to some extent, in the constructions of the general body of members of national and ethnic collectivities and/or citizens of the State; on the other hand, there is always, at least to a certain extent, a separate body of regulations (legal and/or customary) which relate to them specifically as women Yuval-Davis, (1994:187).

An Empowering Nihilism
The title of this section is borrowed from Lawrence Grossberg's (1988) description of postmodern sensibility, which he says 'offers forms of empowerment not only in the face of nihilism but precisely through the forms of nihilism itself'. I want to hold in mind this insight whilst examining the significance of 'rap' culture as analysed in the writings of bell hooks (1994) and Clarence Lusane (1993).

Lusane's article is critical of the enemies of rap who condemn too easily, and draws attention to some of the contradictions inherent in rap culture, describing it as 'a spiralling matrix of empowerment and reaction' (p41). For example, there is no doubt that rap represents an oppositional voice, an expression of frustration, alienation and rebellion which has found a responding echo in marginalised groups worldwide. Its power as cultural protest on a global scale is impressive. At the same time, what has happened to rap is an example of the appropriation of social discontent by the capitalist market, which has packeted and sold it on a global scale in ways which appeal (primarily) to privileged white society, especially males. This is not only incredibly lucrative, but results in a *containment* of the knowledge produced out of the experience of oppression in ways which subvert its 'dangerous' potential. The capitalist enterprise also interprets these experiences in ways which *reinforce* stereotypical and pathologising views of the groups involved. It is expedient for the dominant society to represent these young men as uncivilised and vicious, without taking account of the conditions which have, at least in part, contributed to the phenomenon of rap culture.

For example, evidence quoted by Walker (1995) highlights the speed and scale of social division and the increasing criminalisation of the poor, especially black male youth, in the USA: 'California . . . has raised the number of people incarcerated from 23,000 in 1980 to 125,000 today. . . [and] jails more young black men than South Africa. . .' (p60). Critics of rap usually look at half the picture the rage and sometimes violence contained in the lyrics. What they omit is a simultaneous analysis of *social conditions*, of those who are *interpreters* of rap and the *representations* they support, and those who are potential *consumers* and the commodities they demand.

A related contradiction concerns the way rap has made some young black people rich, both as artists and as businessmen, in the midst of increasing poverty for working class communities, and particularly black communities, in America. Lusane (1993:43) quotes figures which show the official poverty rate for blacks as 32.7% (10.2 million people), which is higher than for Hispanics (28.7%), Asians (13.8%), or whites (11.3%). In October 1992 black teenage unemployment was officially at 42.5%. For many of these young people, rap was not only an opportunity to express anger and frustration, but one of the few economic opportunities open to them to get rich. Lusane suggests that for many rappers, HipHop capitalism promises both riches and racial integrity – they could yell at the system and be paid highly by it at the same time. The contradiction is that they cannot change the economic system that 'is responsible for the misery that forms the substance of the music. . . The commodification of black resistance is not the same as resistance to a society built on commodification' (Lusane 1993:45).

A key impact of rap has been to unveil the conditions of oppression suffered by millions of African-Americans, and by large sections of other minority ethnic groups and poor communities. It has brought to the public gaze the devastating impact of unemployment, drugs and crime, the racist character of the war on drugs and police brutality generally, and the deficiencies of the education system. This laying bare of the conditions of oppression is viewed by Lusane as a 'brilliant exposition of what Foucault has termed the insurrection of subjugated knowledges' (p49). It is an example of the availability of the exercise of power to dominated groups and the fundamental material basis of oppression. At the same time it reveals a misogynist and sexist mentality, particularly in the form of gangsta rap. In some ways this violence against black women can be seen as a self-hatred and therefore consistent with the genre. If this is the case, however, it raises the question of the contradiction between elements of self-hatred and the empowerment which comes from speaking out. Rap music has been condemned as degrading to women, encouraging exploitation of women, sexual harassment and sexual abuse. If as bell hooks (1991) claims, 'part of our struggle for radical black subjectivity is the quest to find ways to construct self and identity that are oppositional and liberatory' (p29), where the most disadvantaged and the poorest are not included, the impact can only be limited. Elsewhere hooks develops an analysis of rap which brings a different insight to the negative elements of the phenomenon (hooks 1994). First she draws attention to the context, by insisting that rap does not appear in a cultural vacuum, but is 'rather expressive of the cultural crossing, mixings, and engagement of black youth culture with the values, attitudes and concerns of the white majority. . . (p116). In other words, the thinking and behaviour that are glorified in gangsta rap are a reflection of the *prevailing* values in society. hooks maintains that they are part of the sexist continuum, necessary for the maintenance of patriarchal social order. She says,

> It is useful to think of misogyny as a field that must be laboured in and maintained both to sustain patriarchy but also to nourish an anti-feminist backlash. And what better group to labour on this plantation' than young black men? (hooks 1994:116).

Given that it is largely young white male consumers who buy and are 'turned on' by this music, hooks sees gangsta rap as not on the margins of American culture but at its centre, as a central core of patriarchy. 'Rather than seeing it as a subversion or disruption of the norm, we . . . need to see it as an *embodiment* of the norm' (p117). hooks raises the question as to how many disenfranchised black males would not surrender to expressing virulent forms of sexism if they knew the rewards would be unprecedented material power and fame. This is not to argue that misogyny should be tolerated or condoned, but to place it in a context which focuses resistance not on the demonisation and destruction of the *messenger* but on the *source* of the exploitative ideology.

Conclusion
Here I want to return to the question I posed at the beginning, that is why is a discourse of empowerment so dominant at this historical moment, and to attempt

to identify strands of an analysis. In this examination of contradictions in the culture of empowerment a number of themes can be identified. First is a theme of containment. Equal Opportunities and affirmative action policies were primarily the bureaucratic response to social unrest. In Britain, uprisings in black communities in the early 1980s forced central and local government to respond. The resultant activities of local authorities resulted in an incorporation of the aspirations of oppressed groups and did not represent a radical reordering of social structures. Indeed, such policies may have resulted in further stigmatisation. Similarly, fundamentalist groups carve out a clear space for women, offer security of role and certainty of belief, but all this is *accommodated* within a narrow framework defined in the interests of patriarchy. The sense of alienation and rage expressed through rap is packaged in a way that transforms it into a commodity and threatens to rob it of its dangerousness. In all these instances a discourse of 'empowerment conceals the continued (albeit in changing forms) class, 'race' and gender exploitation, and works towards containing challenges to such exploitation.

A second, related theme is the talk of empowerment of subordinate groups and the interplay of these groups with hegemonic groups. The character of that interplay is a *collusive* one. Those seeking 'equal opportunities' accept the unequal terms of EO and in return receive resources in competition with other 'oppressed' groups; fundamentalist women accept the roles designed in the interests of men and in return receive certain kinds of recognition; rappers *both* express prevailing values and go along with the commercial packaging of justified anger and in return may receive fame and financial rewards. The culture of empowerment is inextricably bound up with the class, 'race' and gender interests of powerful groups.

A third theme is the location of a discourse of empowerment within existing socially powerful groups. The case of fundamentalist women, when seen as part of a dominant class, illustrates the *construction of empowerment by dominant minorities*. Hindu fundamentalists, the Christian Coalition in the USA, anti-choice campaigners, the New Right in Britain all represent powerful interests. Any examination of empowerment needs to take account of this context. What we have here is not the oppositional agency of the poor and disenfranchised but the enforcement of the concerns of hegemonic groups.

A fourth theme is captured in the Grossberg (1988) quote I referred to earlier: the notion of an *empowering nihilism* – empowerment not only in the face of nihilism but through the forms of nihilism itself. The identity of the Other, attributed to black people, gays and lesbians, disabled people, women, through the process of 'orientalism' Said (1978) is appropriated by young black men (and in different contexts by others) as a clear, strong identity, allowing them to revel in 'the "exoticism", the difference, the uniqueness, and above all the feeling of power that came with it that had been denied them for so long' (Sanghera 1994;42). At the same time Orientalism disrupts this identity by confirming the characteristics displayed by them as of the essence of their alien nature, therefore requiring containment. They are thus kept very neatly in their place in the class and racial hierarchy.

At the same time the contesting of dominant ideologies creates a space where alternative systems of knowledge may be constructed, where other voices may be represented and where social transformation may be possible. One thing is certain, the current culture of empowerment embodies containment and collusion, a depoliticising of action for change, and must be viewed with scepticism as a path to transformation.

References

Ali, Y (1992) Muslim Women and the Politics of Ethnicity and Culture in Northern England, in eds. G Saghal and N Yuval-Davis, *Refusing Holy Orders: Women and Fundamentalism in Britain*, Virago.

Anthias, F. and Yuval-Davis, N. (1993) *Racialized Boundaries: Race, Nation, Gender and Class and the Anti-Racist Struggle*, Routledge.

Campbell, B. (1987) *The Iron Ladies*, Virago.

Craig, G. and Mayo, M. (1995) *Community Empowerment: A Reader in Participation and Development*, Zed Books.

Doyal, L. (1995) *What Makes Women Sick: Gender and the Political Economy of Health*, Macmillan.

Dunant, S. (ed.) (1994) *The War of the Words; the Political Correctness Debate*, Virago.

Foucault, M. (1980), *Power/Knowledge: Selected Interviews and Other Writings*, New York, Pantheon.

Fraser, N. (1995) From Redistribution to Recognition? Dilemmas of Justice in a 'Post-Socialist' Age, in *New Left Review*, 212, July/August 1995.

Gordon, P. (1990) A Dirty War: The New Right and Local Authority Anti-Racism in eds W Ball and J Solomos, *Race and Local Politics*, Macmillan.

Grossberg, L. (1988) Putting the Pop Back in Postmodernism, in ed. A Ross, *Universal Abandon*, University of Minnesota Press.

Hall, S. (1994) Some 'Politically Incorrect' Pathways Through PC, in ed. S Dunant, op.cit. Virago.

hooks, b. (1994) *Outlaw Culture: Resisting Representations,* Routledge.

hooks, b. (1991) *Yearning: Race, Gender and Cultural Politics*, Turnaround Books.

Humphries, B. (1993) 'Are you or have you ever been. . .?' in *Social Work Education*, Vol.12 No.3.

Humphries, B. (1994) Empowerment and Social Research: Elements for an Analytic Framework, in eds. B. Humphries and C. Truman, *Re-thinking Social Research*, Avebury.

Joseph Rowntree Foundation Inquiry Group (1995) Income and Wealth: Report of the JRF Inquiry Group, *Social Policy* Summary, Feb. York, Joseph Rowntree Foundation.

Lusane, C. (1993) Rap, Race and Politics, in *Race and Class*, Vol35, No7.

Maitland, S. (1992) Biblicism, A Radical Rhetoric? in Saghal and Yuval-Davis, op cit.

Mazumdar, S. (1995) Women on the March: Right-wing Mobilization in Contemporary India, in *Feminist Review* 49.

Murray, C. (1990) *The Emerging British Underclass*, London, IEA, Health and Welfare Unit.

Novak, T. (1988) *Poverty and the State: An Historical Sociology*, Open University Press.

Ramazanoglu, C. (1989) *Feminism and the Contradictions of Oppression,* Routledge.

Rutter, M. and Smith, D. J. (1995) *Psychosocial Disorders in Young People*, John Wiley and Sons.

Sahgal, G. (1992) Secular Spaces: the Experience of Asian Women Organizing, in eds G. Sahgal and N. Yuval-Davis, op cit.

Sahgal, G. and Yuval-Davis, N. (1992) *Refusing Holy Orders: Women and Fundamentalism in Britain*, Virago.

Said, E. (1978) *Orientalism*, Peregrine.

Sampson, A. (1995) *Company Man, the Rise and Fall of Corporate Life*, Harper Collins.

Sanghera, P. (1994) Identity Politics and Young 'Asian' *People, Youth and Policy,* Summer.

Spivak, G. C. (1991) Reflections on Cultural Studies in the Post-colonial Conjuncture, in *Critical Studies,* 3 (1): 63-78. Special Issue on *Cultural Studies Crossing Borders.*

Townsend, P. (1993) *The international Analysis of Poverty,* Harvester Wheatsheaf.

Walker, R. (1995) California Rages Against the Dying of the Light, in *New Left Review,* No.209, Jan/Feb, 42-74.

Ward, D. and Mullender, A. (1992), Empowerment and Oppression. an indissoluble pairing for contemporary social work, in *Critical Social Policy,* Issue 32, Autumn, 21-30.

Yuval-Davis, N. (1992) Jewish Fundamentalism and Women's Empowerment, in eds G. Saghal and N. Yuval-Davis, op cit.

Yuval-Davis, N. (1994) Women, Ethnicity and Empowerment, in eds K. K. Bhavnani and A. Phoenix, *Shifting identities Shifting Racisms,* Sage.

Chapter 2
Empowering Sexualities
Jean Carabine

Introduction

In relation to sexuality, empowerment means different things. For some men (and some women) it means having sex when you want it. For feminists it is about rights, safety, autonomy, sexual self-definition and pleasure. For lesbians and gay men, empowerment may include all and some of these aspects alongside the right to be lesbian and gay and to have sex without penalty. The concern of this chapter is with issues of empowerment in relation to sexuality. What can an examination of sexuality tell us about issues of power and strategies for the achievement of empowerment? In this chapter I make a number of assertions. The relationship between sexuality and empowerment can be understood in at least four ways. Further, people seek empowerment in different ways. In terms of the relationship between sexuality and empowerment there is no common agreement about what empowerment might mean in relation to sexuality: empowerment has meant different things and has taken diverse forms. Further, the possibilities for empowerment are bounded by existing discourses of sexuality, difference and identity. The ways in which we understand and explain our sexuality and its relationship with power, influences empowerment strategies. Additionally, difference and identity differentially affect empowerment strategies and their outcomes. In relation to sexuality empowerment does not necessarily involve resistance and can even result in the issue becoming depoliticised. Finally, context affects the possibilities for empowerment. For reasons of clarity these four aspects are dealt with within the text under the headings of meanings, identity and difference, resistance, and context.

An examination of sexuality also reveals that individuals seek empowerment in at least three ways. People achieve empowerment, first, through self-definition and the development of their own social and political identities; second, through sexual practice in personal relations; third, through seeking rights within social institutions and social contexts.

The final section, which raises more questions than answers, considers the capacity of different strategies to speak directly to the politics of empowerment. A feminist-informed Foucauldian analysis (see for example Bartky 1988, Fraser 1989, Braidotti 1991, McNay 1992, Ramazanoglu 1993, Bell 1994) will form the analytical basis for the chapter and the primary focus of discussion will be, in the main, women's experiences of sexuality. Before discussing these various aspects I will first briefly consider how sexuality is popularly understood by way of providing a context for the discussion.

Understanding Sexuality

Sexuality is traditionally and popularly understood as natural and as an essence which is central to our sense of self and identity. Taken for granted as the most natural thing about us, sexuality is assumed to be grounded in the biological, and as such often understood and talked about in terms of genes and hormones. Our desire for sex and sexual expression is similarly explained in terms of a sexual drive, instinct or impulse, beyond control and rationality. This view of sexuality, commonly described as essentialist Weeks (1985), assumes the existence of sexuality as a 'real' essence of human nature, unchanging, biologically innate, universal and an essential aspect of an individual's make-up. This has left us with a legacy of sex as both uncontrollable and unavoidable, requiring satisfaction, control and regulation.

Popularly sexuality is also understood in gendered terms, primarily as, for example, a male sex drive as demonstrated in the idea of men as active sexual agents, naturally sexually initiating, dominant and aggressive. Men are believed to be more highly sexed than women. Correspondingly, women's sexuality is perceived as oppositional yet complementary to male sexuality. Sexually, women are traditionally thought to be more passive, more emotional and thought of as wanting sex for different reasons to men. The dominance of a male-centred sexual discourse is epitomised by Lees's slag/drag dichotomy (1986). If women are sexually active or initiate sex they risk being labelled as 'slags' or 'whores', as 'easy', or unfeminine, even as nymphomaniacs. By contrast it is accepted, even expected, that men will have many sexual relations and initiate sex.

Essentialist informed discourses of sexuality also interact with and are mediated by discourses of 'race', disability and class to produce differentiating effects. For example, racist ideas about black, especially African-Caribbean, women produce images of black women as sexually voracious, lacking sexual control, and of Asian women sexualised as erotic, exotic and passive. Disabled women are seen as incapable of sex, without sexuality and/or as sexually vulnerable requiring supervision and control.

In the preceding paragraphs I have tended to focus on the impact of essentialist ideas about sexuality as they have influenced popular understandings of sexuality. In real life the experience of both popular discourse and material encounters is more complicated and contradictory than this. The perception of women as sexually passive is neither even nor consistent. Popularly, there is equally an expectation, as evidenced in many women's magazines, that women will be sexually active and assertive possessing 'equal rights' to sexual pleasure and fulfilment with men. This is all in pursuit of even better heterosexual sex. This is not a direct challenge to passivity so much as representing new ways of providing pleasure. Traditional/popular discourse is contradictory so that whilst it assumes passivity it may also encourage a model of female dominance' to meet certain male fantasies of wanting to be seduced. Correspondingly, social attitude surveys reveal that homosexuality is more acceptable than in the past. Whilst popular culture romances with 'lipstick' lesbians and lesbian chic (Hamer and Budge 1994) discrimination against and the abuse of lesbian and gay men persists (Pink Paper 26 May 1995[1]). At an individual level people understand, explain and experience their sexuality in uneven, contradictory and complex ways. The material experience of their sexuality(ies) is informed by but often at odds with the discursive representations of that sexuality.

It is also assumed to be 'natural' and 'normal' that the direction of a person's sexuality – their sexual drive – will he towards the opposite sex. In this sense, sexuality is traditionally seen as a heterosexual drive and the normative means of fulfilment is through penile-vaginal intercourse. Therefore, not only is 'natural' sex heterosexual but it is also considered 'natural' to want heterosexual sex. By comparison lesbianism and homosexuality are popularly conceived of as not 'normal' and often as 'unnatural' and perverse.

Sexuality is also commonly regarded as intimately a personal and private matter. A pervasive belief is that what individuals do sexually whether on their own or with others is primarily their own business provided they do not affect or harm others[2]. However, this view of sexuality as private is contradicted in a number of ways. First, what people do sexually, where and with whom, is the focus of implicit and explicit social regulation and control. Foucault has demonstrated that sexuality rather than being secret and repressed in the Victorian era was very much a matter of public concern and discourse (Foucault 1990). Second, challenges to the established 'truths' of sexuality and related analyses of the relationship between sexuality and power, from, amongst others, feminist, lesbian and gay activists, postmodernism and queer theory and activism have brought the issue of sexuality very much into the public domain. Finally, despite a strong belief in sexuality as personal, private and beyond the boundaries of state intervention it is a focus of political and public discourse. Having set the context for the discussion I will now explore what sexuality can tell us about empowerment.

Sexuality and Empowerment
Using sexuality as a basis for exploring empowerment I suggest that as individuals we can seek empowerment in four ways. For the purposes of clarity these are listed as though they were discrete and separate. In practice individuals may seek empowerment in one or more of these ways coterminously as well as at different levels,

for example, individually and/or collectively, within each of these. Returning to the ways in which individuals seek empowerment: first, we can seek it in relation to our own subjectivity – in relation to how we define and enact our own sexuality/sexualities. In short, the embodiment of self-identity achieved through sexuality. Second, we may seek empowerment through sexual practice on a one-to-one (or more) basis. Third, we may seek empowerment through demands for individual and collective 'rights' in relation to various social contexts and institutions. A fourth strategy is the refusal to accept, and even the transgressing of, existing sexual and gender categorization and definitions so that current and prevalent notions of gender and sexuality are rejected and reconstituted.

The above framework informs the discussion in the following sections which, due to the constraints of space, focuses primarily on different sexuality empowerment strategies in order to see what insight they can provide on possibilities and limitations of empowerment.

Sexuality and the Possibilities for Empowerment
In this section I shall focus on three of the four aspects which in the introduction I suggested affect the possibilities for empowerment. These are meanings, identity and difference, and resistance. These aspects will be considered next. The fourth, context, will be discussed in the section on the limits of empowerment.

Empowerment and the Meanings of Sexuality
In relation to sexuality, empowerment has meant different things. Different approaches to explaining and understanding sexuality and sexual relations advocate different political and empowerment strategies. For radical feminism it has meant an emphasis upon women gaining control over their bodies, as in demands for sexual self-definition, access to abortion and contraception, and demands for reproductive rights. For libertarian feminism it has also meant the right to pleasure in sex, and for the lesbian and gay movement it has in addition meant being visible and having equal rights with heterosexuals to sex and to services. How we understand and explain sexuality has important implications for the possibility of empowerment and strategies for change. How we might conceptualize empowerment in relation to sexuality is affected, even limited, by contemporary discourses of sexuality and heterosexuality and the assumptions they contain about what is sex, the nature of sexual relations and normality of heterosexuality.

The conception of sexuality as being determined by nature has resulted in some lesbian women and gay men seeking equal rights and empowerment on a 'sex as nature' basis arguing that it is unfair to discriminate against a person on the basis of a sexuality with which they were born and over which they have no control. For some, the attraction of this stance is that it offers a sense of belonging and certainty, as well as a basis from which moral conservatism can he challenged. This conception has also resulted in biological explanations, and even 'cures', for homosexuality as in the search for the existence of the 'gay gene' as in the work of Simon Le Vay, who is himself gay (1991, 1993). Similarly, essentialist ideas about sexuality are evident in some radical feminist strategies for sexual empowerment as with the belief that an essential sexual 'true' femininity and 'real' self will be revealed once women are 'freed' of male domination and male definitions of female sexuality.

Similarly, aspects of a liberatory approach to sexual empowerment, for example, the idea of sex as personal choice, result in particular empowerment outcomes. Research undertaken by the Women, Risk and AIDS Project (WRAP) found that some young women's model of sexual empowerment was based on a 'male' model of sexuality in that they sought freedom to have sex without obligation. This, WRAP argue, 'disguises inequalities of power and control in sexual rela-tionships with a liberal discourse of personal choice' (Holland, Ramazanoglu, Scott, Sharpe and Thomson 1991:12). As Holland *et al* suggest, this model of sexuality is particularly powerful and enticing for young women who are attempt-ing to control their lives and who wish to reject passive female sexuality.

Furthermore, demands for women's greater sexual pleasure and fulfilment on a par with those of male sexuality have their limitations and have often been achieved only within permissible boundaries. Taking the question of limitations first, the demand for freedom of sexual expression which characterizes libertarian feminist empowerment strategies stems from an idea of sex as repressive and a philosophy which identifies sexual freedom as a route to liberation. In calling for sexual freedom libertarian feminists have been criticised for individualizing sexuality and in doing so of ignoring the relationship between sexuality and power. In the pursuit of sexual freedom through pleasure 'they regard the release of female sexual energy as more important than the restraint of male sexuality. Therefore, they resist drawing lines between safe and dangerous, and politically correct and incorrect sex' (Sawicki 1988:179).

The realisation of women's demands for sexual pleasure and fulfilment has not been achieved without limits. Jeffreys (1985) points out that, historically, women's newly identified sexual desire and 'right' to sexual fulfilment were constituted in the work of nineteenth-century sexologists within a heterosexual frame. In this period, women were still expected to comply with their husband's desires and to be more sexually responsive within heterosexual sex. In the sexual revolution of the permissive 1960s women won the 'right' to enjoy sex on equal terms with men. However, it has also been suggested that 'the ideology of sexual liberation was little more that a thinly veiled manoeuvre by men to keep women socially subordinate' (Seidman 1992:97) and had more to do with meeting male sexual desires and needs. Additionally, the dangers and risks for women associated with non-marital and unattached no-obligation sex were rarely acknowledged. This model which again privileged heterosexual sex and vaginal intercourse sex both contained and limited the possibilities for sexual empowerment within a heterosexual frame. It is also unlikely that such models which privileged heterosexual sex could be said to be empowering for lesbian or celibate women. This continuing theme can be found in the prevalent and popular discourses of today's female sexuality. Forbes (1994:5) suggests that contemporary discourses of sexuality demand that women express their sexual desire without inhibition or constraint as a means of self-expression. 'The difference today, . . . is that women are constructed as eager, desiring subjects and willing participants, who, in order to express themselves, are turning themselves into erotic objects of sexual consumption for men' (op cit). Forbes argues that, whilst '[w]omen may have greater self-expression within heterosexuality . . . the regulatory effects of this discourse ensure that women continue to be made available and subject to male desire. Liberating female sexuality allows men greater sexual access to women' (Forbes 1994:11). However, this argument is in danger of positioning women as passive dupes lacking agency.

Different feminist approaches to explaining and understanding sexuality, sexual relations and power have, then, advocated different political and empowerment strategies. A key aspect of feminist analyses of sexuality has been to challenge many of the taken-for-granted assumptions about the naturalness of male/female relations, and particularly of heterosexuality. Feminists (see, for example, MacKinnon 1982 and Hanmer and Maynard 1987) have critiqued heterosexuality as a form and expression of male power over women based in male/female sexual relations. In challenging traditional ideas about the 'naturalness' of sexuality and sexual relations, feminists such as Jackson (1978 & 1982) and Vance (1989) have argued instead that sexuality is socially constructed; that sexuality is socially, historically and culturally variable. Many feminists would see sexuality as fundamental to the construction and maintenance of power relations between men and women although they would be likely to disagree as to the specific locus of sexuality in the oppression of women, or about the processes by, and through which sexuality is constructed. Sexuality is perceived as either the primary means through which men have power over women or it is less significant than, or equivalent to, class or the sexual division of labour. However, there are similarities in the way that power is perceived of in relation to sexuality. Generally, feminism has conceptualised power as a fixed dynamic centrally located on a gender/sex axis or on hetero-patriarchy through which men have power which they exercise over women (Ramazanoglu 1993:92-5). As a result women have struggled for change and challenged male power in their individual relationships with men and within wider society.

These different conceptual positions have resulted in distinct empowerment strategies. The radical feminist project primarily sought empowerment and change through separatist working and politics, the building of a separate women's culture which would facilitate, particularly for those radical feminists identified as cultural feminists, the enhancement and 'freeing' of 'true' femininity and female sexuality based on female values, with women's control of their bodies and over their sexuality being given a high priority. Heterosexuality was seen as the pivotal domain in women's struggle for change and liberation. Many radical feminists believe that radical transformation would not be achieved through economic, social or legal reforms alone but that 'women had to free them-selves from male-imposed identities and roles and struggle against the institution of heterosexuality' (Seidman 1992:102). By comparison socialist feminists sought empowerment through challenging class relations and the socially con-structed sexual division of labour in the labour market and the home. Both women's liberation and socialism are joint goals although, as Williams (1989:62-63) points out, the two often conflict. The state was seen as reinforcing women's position in the home while capital demands cheap labour from women usually, but not always, outside the home. The major focus of socialist feminists for action and change has tended to be the Labour Party, trade unions and local government, for example as with campaigns for abortions and against sexual harassment.

Identity and Difference
This examination of sexuality and empowerment reveals that not only does how we understand and explain sexuality have implications for empowerment possibilities but also that empowerment outcomes are mediated and affected by the significance and experience of difference. People as individuals have multi-identities and as such hold different agendas for change and various positions at the same and different times and in different contexts. We cannot assume that empowerment will mean the same thing for different people or even for the same people at all times and in differing contexts. To do so would require assuming universal needs, outcomes and participation in relation to empowerment strategies. That an individ-ual engages in a particular sexual behaviour does not mean that that individual will

identify with any sexual identity or categorisation attached to it. For example, it does not follow that men who have sex with men will identify as gay.

Many continue to identify as heterosexual (Humphreys, 1971; Davies *et al* 1993). It cannot, therefore, be assumed that they would seek or demand empowerment in the same way as men who identify as gay.

Correspondingly, what may be experienced as empowering for one group of women may not necessarily be experienced as such by other women as with demands for greater sexual freedom which privilege heterosexual sex and vaginal intercourse (see above). In developing strategies it is important to be aware of this and to avoid universalising claims and recognise the impact of difference on such claims. For example, white women's claims for access to abortion and sterilisation have been criticised by black women who felt that they had always had enforced abortions, sterilisations and contraception because of racialised ideas about their sexuality. The lesbian and gay appeal to a notion of identity based on 'sex as nature' which is discussed above is problematic not only because it produces a static, fixed and individualistic model of identity but also because, as (Butler 1990:2) comments, identity premised on such grounds is constituted by the very discourse it seeks to challenge. Foucault is equally sceptical of liberation politics rooted in identity politics where those identities arise out of categorisations of the individual which attaches them to their sexual identity and which is founded on the discourse which they seek to challenge (Foucault in Sawicki 1988:183). Second, if we accept that neither 'woman' nor 'lesbian' is a unitary subject and that each of us is multi-situated with sometimes competing, conflicting and contradictory multiple identities which are anything but fixed being constituted through a range of social relationships then, as Sawicki (1988:184-5), suggests,

> An understanding of sexual liberation based on this latter notion of identity, one that is a product of social relations and conflicts, requires more than a demand for the right to one's sexuality, for, on this model, one's 'sexuality' is a matter of socially and historically specific practices and relationships that are contingent and dynamic, and thus a matter of political struggle. In such a model of identity, freedom is not something following from a notion of one's true nature or essence as a 'human being', 'woman', or proletarian', but rather our capacity to choose the forms of experience through which we constitute ourselves.

At the same time, it is possible to see how groups who were categorised as 'other', as deviant and abnormal because of their sexuality, have sought empowerment through demonstrating that they are subjects with agency claiming a positive identity out of a negative categorisation. In this way being lesbian or gay (this is also true of other 'empowered' groups such as black and disabled people) is a positive identity constructed out of, and through the experience, of oppression. The idea of identity as a part of resistance is important because 'the assertion of identity is a process people can relate to because it reclaims agency and makes them feel powerful' (Aziz 1992:302). Similarly, where individuals and groups take on the categorisation as a positive identity, and claim it for themselves and in the process redefine it, this challenges the prevalent meaning expressed in the discourse. Underscoring this approach is the implicit notion of empowerment through a politics *of* identity in contrast to 'Queer' strategies that advocate a politics *against* identity. Queer strategies call for a destabilising of identity as the basis for social and political empowerment. On the one band, because a politics based on a 'fixed identity position privileges those for whom that position is the primary or only marked identity' (Duggan 1994:4) which in lesbian and gay politics usually means white, middle class and male. On the other, gay identity as it is currently constructed reinforces hetero-normativity and the prevalent hetero/homosexual code (Seidman 1993:130). The ultimate aim of Queer theory and activism is the eventual destabilising of identity as fixed and unitary[3] However, this approach can be criticised amongst other things for ignoring the importance of identity in resistance (see Aziz 1992, Seidman 1993) and because, as Fraser argues, 'in order to eventually destabilize the homo-hetero dichotomy, it must first mobilize "queers"' (1995:83).

Resistance and Empowerment

In this section I shall explore the relationship between empowerment and resistance. Resistance can be thought of in different ways. Commonly, it is understood in association with relations of power. Foucault suggests that where there is power the possibility for resistance exists. As with power which is present everywhere so resistance is possible at multiple points (Sawicki 1991:23-4). Ramazanoglu and Holland (1993:240) point out that, in feminist analyses of gendered power relations, women have agency because 'feminist notions of heterosexual relations conceive of power in terms of the possibility of women resisting men's sexual domination and so empowering themselves'. That women are conceptualised as having agency within a matrix where men have power is important because it allows the possibility for resistance – 'through the theory that men "hold" power over women and that women can identify this power and collectively resist it' (Ramazanoglu and Holland, 1993:241).

However we may conceive of resistance and of power relations the relationship between resistance, power and empowerment is complex. To be empowered does not of itself necessitate that we either 'resist' or challenge existing power relations. Nor does it require that we establish a counter discourse. Empowerment does not necessarily have to involve resistance through '*resisting*' but instead empower-ment may be achieved through 'embracing' existing power structures as in equal rights demands to same-sex marriages or for 'gays in the military'. Often political struggles around sexuality have adopted an equal rights stance as the challenge to sexism and heterosexuality. Equal rights approaches have focused on obtaining the same privileging as heterosexual relations with campaigners demanding, for example, the right to marriage and legal recognition and public validation of same-sex relationships; along with the right to parent and have children. However, I would suggest that the problem with this approach is not only is the privileged position of heterosexuality not resisted in that it is not called into question but any differences are ignored or even denied. Phelan (1994:2) suggests that arguing that lesbians or gay men are equal or potentially the same as heterosexuals fails to challenge heterosexuality. Such demands for equal rights are based on claims for an equal share of power.

Neither does resistance always result in empowerment. A woman may resist being raped but still end up being raped. Being intellectually empowered, choosing to use a contraceptive, seeking sexual pleasure and fulfilment or demanding equal rights may not always involve a process of resisting. Perhaps one way of understanding the relationship between empowerment and resistance is to visualise different levels of resistance (such as individual, subjective, social and political, etc) which have different outcomes (temporary, individual, material, collective, subjective and transformative) and to recognise that resistance in any one area does not guarantee empowerment in either that or any other area, or in subsequent engagements. Neither does empowerment at an individual level result in collective empowerment or social change. Neither resistance nor empowerment may result in a change in power relations

To some my argument might seem crude but what I am attempting to illustrate is that the notion of resistance is problematic and the relationship between resistance and power complex. On the one hand, demands for equal rights with heterosexuals may not necessarily challenge the privileged and powerful position of heterosexuality. On the other, lesbians and gay men who adopt this strategy can be seen to be resisting heterosexuality merely by identifying as lesbian and gay.

Similarly, it can be argued that for women to use contraception, or be intellectually empowered or to seek sexual fulfilment may involve resistance – at the level of resisting disciplinary power through resistance to prevalent discourses. But if the discourse of female sexuality now means that it is generally acceptable in most western social contexts (except in certain religious ones, e.g. Catholic) for women to use the contraceptive pill does this still therefore involve resistance particularly when this does not require or involve negotiation with male partners? What this discussion reveals is that there is a need for a critical understanding of resistance to be incorporated within critiques of empowerment.

Empowerment can take many forms. In feminist analyses of sexuality, particularly those written by heterosexual women, there has been until recently a reluctance to critique and problematise heterosexuality. This shift has been the result of pressure from, in the main, lesbian feminists. What is interesting about this example is, firstly, it reveals that empowerment imposes a responsibility on those who disempower alongside a commitment to change. This responsibility is different from the ideas of 'enabling' central to traditional notions and uses of empowerment. Instead, the example of sexuality reveals that in this context empowerment imposes a duty to question and problematise our own subject position. Marilyn Frye argues that heterosexual women need to become continually aware that they are heterosexual and that they recognise the privileges of their position (Frye 1983). The achievement of empowerment does not have to result, as is often argued in a relinquishing of power on the behalf of the empowered or the powerful.

Sexuality and the Limits of Empowerment
Many factors could probably be identified as limiting possibilities for empowerment. In this section I shall focus on three of these which arise in relation to sexuality. First, empowerment once gained cannot be perceived as a fixed possession, or as something which will necessarily result in a change in existing power relations. Instead, it should be understood as something which requires continual negotiation. Second, empowerment may result in a depoliticisation of sexuality issues, such as with 'lesbian chic'. Third, context can be seen to affect empowerment possibilities and outcomes.

Negotiating the Parameters of Empowerment
In looking at sexuality we can see that empowerment is not necessarily a transferable commodity: once achieved it is not permanently retained. Rather, empowerment can be seen to be a dynamic which has to be constantly and continually negotiated and this is particularly the case in individual sexual relations. That women may successfully negotiate sex on their own terms in one relationship does

not ensure that this is guaranteed in each and every subsequent sexual engagement with either a specific individual or with subsequent partners. On each occasion, sex on this basis may have to be newly negotiated. Similarly, WRAP's work with young women illustrates that whilst women can be empowered intellectually this does not guarantee safer sex. What this research illustrates is that it is not enough to be knowledgeable about sex, or to be sexually self-aware or even to define one's own sexuality, because this does not in itself guarantee a shift in inequality in sexual relations. A woman can be determined and have powerful intentions but these do not ensure her sexual safety or that her sexual 'needs' will be met in practice – or that her sexual desires will be considered (Holland *et al* 1991).

What this and the WRAP research (as well as critiques of libertarian approaches) show is that empowerment does not necessarily result in a shift in power relations. It may be empowering for a woman to have control over her body in respect of reproduction but it does not necessarily result in a corresponding change in power relations because her male partner is not necessarily involved in any negotiation about the use of contraception[4]. This suggests, first, that individual empowerment does not of itself require to be part of a negotiated social relation. Second, that individual empowerment does not necessarily result in a shift in power relations and, therefore, that empowerment could be said to be limited or even that it is not empowerment. Third, as suggested above, empowerment outcomes can be realised without resistance.

'Lesbian Chic': Empowerment through Depoliticisation

Recently, there has been an apparent acceptance of lesbian and gay sexuality partic-ularly in the form of 'lesbian chic'. More programmes either about lesbian and gay sexuality or including lesbian and gay male characters appear on TV than ever before, for example Gaytime TV (BBC2), 'Out' and 'Dyke TV' (C4), the emergence of lesbian and gay characters in numerous soaps and other pro-grammes – Eastenders (BBC 1), Brookside (C4), Emmerdale Farm (ITV), Portrait of a Marriage (BBC 2). Oranges Are Not The Only Fruit (BBC I) and Between the Lines (BBC I). As Hamer and Budge (1994:2) confirm, 'popular culture has been increasingly important as a discursive site for lesbian and feminist politics'. This apparent acceptance and greater mainstream visibility of lesbians could be viewed positively as empowering for lesbians or more cynically as the depoliticisation of lesbianism whereby lesbianism is presented as personal lifestyle choice rather than a radical political position. This may be experienced as empowering for the individual but it remains as very much an individual sexual preference, sexual liberation through the right to sexual fulfil-ment and personal choice rather than a challenge to the privileging of heterosexuality. Certainly, and as Hamer and Budge (1994:11) argue, 'part of lesbianism's new acceptability has been as a result of lesbian-feminist political struggles; given this, it is ironic that lesbianism's entree into the mainstream has been at the expense of a politicised version of lesbian identity' (it may also be that the nature of political resistance has shifted). Forbes (1994:10) argues that 'lesbianism as a radical alternative to heterosexuality is depoliticised and neutralised within the individualism of personal choice and fulfilment'. She goes on to suggest that 'the boundaries which demarcate what is possible, desirable and acceptable within heterosexuality are extended now to include a depoliticized lesbianism and the sexual demands and expression of women' (ibid). Thus empowerment at this individual level can result in incorporation or even in a form of co-option into and by the mainstream. Lesbians may experience this mainstream attention as empowering but it also results in lesbianism being depoliticised.

Empowering Contexts
Contexts affect the meanings of empowerment in relation to sexuality as the following example illustrates. The sexual revolution of the 1960s sought liberation from repressive sexuality through the pursuit of pleasure and sexual freedom to have sex - when, where, as often as you wanted and with as many partners as you desired. But the impact of AIDS has altered what is possible in relation to sexual empowerment in this context. Sexual freedom here is sought at the risk of death unless safer sex is practised. As Linda Singer (1993:116-117) argues, '[t]he age of sexual epidemic demands a new sexual politics, and therefore a rethinking of the relationship between bodies, pleasures, and powers beyond the call for liberation from repression'.

In another essay Singer(1993:65) argues that the onset of AIDS has 'redefined the site of struggle in the politics of pleasure' which has produced a reconsideration of priorities. To illustrate this Singer (1993:66) takes as an example the decision to close the San Franciscan 'bathhouses' as a means of controlling the spread of AIDS. The bathhouses had been a key site of gay political mobilisation Closure of the baths was opposed on the grounds that it was not just the health of individuals that was at risk but also 'the very gains gays had made in securing social and symbolic space free from intervention and regulation from the state' (bid).

What this reveals is that empowerment is affected by context. So the site of empowerment, in this case the bathhouses, can be seen as empowering a pre-AIDS epidemic and as dangerous in a different context – the AIDS epidemic. Additionally, this illustrates further the complexity of the notion of empowerment – the dangerousness of the bathhouses did not stop them being a site of political struggle. In a related vein, empowerment strategies may not be successful in other contexts. The distribution of condoms and spermicides are widely accepted as the main means of ensuring safer sex. But as Singer (1993:67) reports Margaret Sangar was imprisoned for attempting to distribute condoms to women who were dying from illegal abortions and from childbirth.

Conclusion

Empowerment, particularly in health and social welfare literature, is usually understood to mean 'to give a voice to, to enable, and developing individuals' ability to help themselves'. It is variously described as being about citizenship, rights, responsibilities and needs. Expressed in terms of 'having a say', user involvement, exercising power and control, taking charge and sometimes in terms of changing society but more usually it is about changing the individual. However, an analysis of sexuality reveals that empowerment may be understood in both similar and different but more complex ways.

First, there is no common agreement about what empowerment might mean in relation to sexuality issues. It can mean sexual freedom, greater visibility, equal rights, control over our bodies and sexuality, fighting discrimination, transgressing sexual norms or better sex. Possible meanings of strategies for empowerment are influenced by existing discourses, not only of sexuality, but also, for example, by discourses of race, gender, disability, and class, as well as analyses of power. We need to be cognisant that the possibilities for empowerment are affected and even limited by, in the case of sexuality, contemporary discourses of sexuality and the assumptions contained in them about what are 'normal' and 'natural' and appropriate and acceptable sexual relations.

Second, and relatedly, difference and identity differentially impact on empowerment strategies and outcomes. Individuals are multi-positioned having different co-existing identities which influence their choice of strategies for change adopted at specific moments and in particular contexts. It follows therefore that individuals may seek empowerment in certain contexts and not others and for different reasons.

Third, it is not necessary for individuals to resist, challenge or change existing relations of power in order to experience empowerment. Correspondingly, empowerment can also result in a depoliticisation of sexuality issues or sexual identities as in the example of 'lesbian chic'. In order to understand empowerment we need, therefore, also to know more about meanings and contexts of resistance and relations of power. Empowerment is not about gaining power: rather there exists a more complex and contradictory relationship between the two. We do and do not have power in different circumstances, in the same contexts but at different moments. What is important is recognizing the workings of power and our own relationship to it.

Fourth, understanding empowerment requires that we take into consideration the social, political and historical context within which discourses about empowerment take place.

I have suggested that possibilities for empowerment are influenced by meanings, identity and context and that empowerment does not necessarily involve resistance or result in a change in existing power relations; indeed, empowerment may also result in a sexuality issue becoming depoliticised. Similarly, individuals seek empowerment in different ways and on different levels at one and the same time; this also affects empowerment possibilities.

As I suggested above there are no agreed and universal definitions of empowerment. The critique offered in this chapter by no means provides clear answers but instead is a contribution to a more critical understanding of empowerment.

I would like to thank Fiona Williams for her helpful and constructive comments on an earlier draft of this chapter

Notes

[1] A country-wide survey of gays and heterosexuals undertaken by Social and Community Planning Research revealed that 70% of heterosexuals thought it 'quite natural' to be gay or lesbian, 44% said they would object to gay men being employed in schools and 33% said they would be less likely to employ gay or lesbian applicants (Pink Paper 26 May 1995).

[2] This approach is one adopted in the 1957 Wolfenden Report on male homosexuality and prostitution. The report distinguishes between what should be allowed in public and what should be tolerated in private.

[3] For a more detailed discussion see for example Seidman 1993, Warner 1993, Duggan 1994 and Frazer 1995.

[4] From another perspective it can be argued women's access to contraception and abortion means that they do not have to submit to the inevitability of motherhood or reproduction and it permits the possibility of separating sex from reproduction for women and therefore of empowerment. It also permits the possibility of another discourse of resistance to 'truth' of sexuality.

31

References
Aziz, R. (1992) 'Feminism and the challenge of racism: deviance or difference ?' in H. Crowley and S. Himmelweit (eds) *Knowing Women: Feminism and Knowledge*. Cambridge: Polity Press in association with the Open University.

Bartky, S. (1988) 'Foucault, Femininity, and the Modernization of Patriarchal Power' in I. Diamond and L. Quinby (eds) *Feminism and Foucault Reflections on Resistance*. Boston: Northeastern University Press.

Bell, V (1994) *Interrogating Incest Feminism*, Foucault and the law. London: Routledge.

Braidotti, R. (1991) *Patterns of Dissonance: A Study of Women in Contemporary Philosophy*. Cambridge: Polity Press.

Butler, J. (1990) *Gender Trouble: Feminism and the Subversion of Identity* London: Routledge

Davies, PM.; Hickson, F.C.I.; Weatherburn, P. and Hunt, A.J. (1993) *AIDS Sex, Gay men and AIDS* London: The Falmer Press.

Duggan, L. (1994) 'Queering the State' in *Social Text*. Summer, pp 1-14.

Evans, D. (1993) *Sexual Citizenship: The Material Construction of Sexualities*. London: Routledge.

Forbes, J. (1994) 'Punishing Sex: Disciplining Women in Contemporary Discourses of Sexuality' *Sexualities in Context*, Preston: British Sociological Association Conference.

Foucault, M. (1990) *The History of Sexuality, Volume 1: An Introduction*. New York: Vintage Books.

Fraser, N. (1989) *Unruly Practices: Power Discourse and Gender in Contemporary Social Theory*. Cambridge: Polity Press.

Fraser, N. (1995) 'From Distribution to Recognition? Dilemmas of Justice in a 'Post-Socialist" Age' in *New Left Review*, No. 212, July/August, pp.68-93.

Frye, M. (1983) *The Politics of Reality: Essays in Feminist Theory*. New York: The Crossing Press.

Hamer, D. and Budge, B. (1994) (eds) *The Good, The Bad and The Gorgeous: Popular Culture's Romance with Lesbianism*. London: Pandora.

Hanmer, J. and Maynard, M. (1987) 'Violence and Gender Stratification' in J. Hanmer and M. Maynard (eds) *Women, Violence and Social Control.* Basingstoke: British Sociological Association/Macmillan.

Hewitt, M. (1992) *Welfare Ideology and Need: Developing Perspectives on the Welfare State.* Brighton: Harvester Wheatsheaf.

Holland, J.; Ramazanoglu, C.; Scott, S.; Sharpe, S. and Thomson, R. (1991) *Pressure, resistance, empowerment: Young women and the negotiation of safer sex.* WRAP paper 6, London: the Tufnell Press.

Humphreys, L. (1971) *Tea Room Trade.* London: Duckworth.

Jackson, S. (1978) *On the Social Construction of Female Sexuality.* London: Women's Research and Resources Centre.

Jackson, S. (1982) 'Femininity, Masculinity and Sexuality' in S. Freidman and E. Sarah (eds) *On The Problem of Men: Two Feminist Conferences.* London: Women's Press.

Jackson, S. (1994) 'Heterosexuality as a Problem for Feminist Theory' *Sexualities in Context*, Preston: British Sociological Association Conference.

Jeffreys, S. (1985) *The Spinster and Her Enemies: Feminism and Sexuality 1880-1930.* London: Pandora Press.

Lees, S. (1986) *Losing Out: Sexuality and Adolescent Girls.* London; Hutchinson Education.

Le Vay, S. (1991) 'The Gay Gene' in *Science.* 253, pp.1034-7.

Le Vay, S (1993) *The Sexual Brain.* Boston: Mass. Institute of Technology Press.

MacKinnon, (1982) 'Feminism, Marxism, Method and the State' in S. Harding (ed) *Feminism and Methodology.* Milton Keynes: Indiana/Open University Presses.

McNay, L.(1992) *Foucault and Feminism: Power Gender and Self.* Cambridge: Polity Press.

Phelan, S. (1994) *Getting Specific; Postmodern Lesbian Politics.* Minneapolis: University of Minnesota Press.

Ramazanoglu, C. (1993) (ed) *Up Against Foucault: Explorations of some tensions between Foucault and feminism.* London: Routledge.

Ramazanoglu, C. and Holland, J. (1993) 'Women's sexuality and men's appropriation of desire' in C. Ramazanoglu (1993) (ed) Up *Against Foucault: Explorations of some tensions between Foucault and feminism*. London: Routledge.

Sawicki, J. (1988) 'Identity Politics and Sexual Freedom: Foucault Feminism' in I. Diamond and L. Quinby (eds) *Feminism and Foucault: Reflections on Resistance*. Boston: Northeastern University Press.

Sawicki, J. (1991) *Disciplining Foucault: Feminism, Power, and the Body*. New York: Routledge.

Seidman, S. (1992) *Embattled Eros: Sexual Politics and Ethics in Contemporary America*. New York: Routledge.

Seidman, S. (1993) 'Identity and Politics in a "Postmodern" Gay Culture: Some Historical and Conceptual Notes' in M. Warner (ed) *Fear of a Queer Planet: Queer Politics and Social Theory*. Minneapolis: University of Minnesota Press.

Singer, L. (1993) *Erotic Welfare: Sexual Theory and Politics in the Age of Epidemic*. New York: Routledge.

Vance, C. (1989) 'Social Construction Theory: Problems in the History of Sexuality' in D. Altman, C. Vance, M. Vinicus and J.Weeks (eds) *Homosexuality, Which Homosexuality?* Amsterdam/London: Uitgeverij An Dekker-Schorer/Gay Men's Press.

Warner, M. (ed) *Fear of a Queer Planet: Queer Politics and Social Theory*. Minneapolis: University of Minnesota Press.

Weeks, J. (1985) *Sexuality and Its Discontents: Meanings, Myths and Modern Sexualities*. London: Routledge.

Williams, F. (1989) *Social Policy: A Critical Introduction*. Cambridge: Polity Press.

Chapter 3
The Marginal Politics of Our Bodies?
Women's Health, the Disability Movement, and Power

Janet Price

The prospect of writing an essay about empowerment and the body filled me with anxiety and I approached putting words to paper with a high degree of ambivalence. I felt unqualified to write about it, and as I tried to work out why, I recognised that it was because I had an increasing suspicion that the concept of empowerment did not apply to me, that my experience of my body over the last six years, during which I have been living with illness and have experienced disability, had somehow disqualified me. My 'broken body'[1] appeared to exclude me from the realm of power, both materially – I have had to stop work and with this both my income and my status have fallen – and theoretically. I felt there was no longer any point in my aspiring to join those who had become 'empowered', for implicit within the idea of empowerment is a sense that power is something that can be gained and held, and it is only those with bodies that are potentially whole, stable and strong who can aspire to such power. Modern notions of power are bound up with masculinity, with bodily competence, and these inform an unspecified but ever-present ideal, that of the fully realised, physically perfect, white, masculine subject, against which all else is measured and found wanting. Of course the irony is that it is those who in some way will never match this ideal, those on the margins, for whom empowerment may be most crucial.

However, against my feeling that empowerment is predicated on an unbroken body is the widely held thesis that modern notions of power 'have denied the reality of the body in favour of the soul, consciousness and ideology' (Foucault 1980:57). In the first section, I will address this seeming paradox – by which modern power can be seen both to deny the body and, simultaneously, to demand a perfect body as its precondition - and will explore the implications of this for the politics of movements such as women's health and disability.

Even as I argue that so many are excluded from the possibility of empowerment through their marginal embodiment, I recognise that such terms as 'emancipation' and 'empowerment are problematic in themselves. As Lather suggests, one of the characteristics of the subject of emancipatory pedagogy is the need to know 'the world in order to set herself free from it' (1991:141). The demand is for an outside view, divorced from the material ties of the world and of flesh. And yet power is not only *represented* by the material, by the trappings of wealth and possessions, but is itself perceived *to be*, at some level, material. Within both liberal and Marxist thought, power is conceived of as something which is held or possessed by individuals (or groups/classes), and, as Gatens argues, 'both philosophies assume that power is principally manifested in the regulation and control of politico-economic relations' whether, as in the liberal view, for legitimate use by representatives of the sovereign or State within the public sphere or, as in the Marxist view, originating in economic relations and used by one class to oppress another (Gatens 1992: 123). The material forms of power thus relate directly to the economic and political. Within Marxist thought, power is also held to be ideological, exercised through State apparatuses such as schools, the medical system and the family. Whilst the relationship between the material/ideological binary in Marxist thought and the mind/matter dichotomy of liberal humanism is complex, Gatens suggests that what they reveal is the inability of both liberal and Marxist theories 'to address the issue of corporeal specificity in any terms other than those of biological "facts" or ideology' (1992:127) as, for example, in the opposition of biological 'sex' and socially constructed 'gender'. For an understanding of these oppositions, we can look back to the metaphysics of the European Enlightenment.

Power and the body
Pre-modern thought tied authority to the body in specific ways, power being manifest either in the body of the sovereign (Foucault 1980) or in a sublimated form, through representations of the body of God, both of which evoked a patriarchal order. The position people occupied in society was pre-ordained and structured through religion, heredity and the mechanisms of the legal/juridical system. Scheman suggests, 'the way people knew their places in the world had to do with their bodies and the histories of those bodies' (1993:186), which in turn informed their view of themselves as part of some greater, hierarchically ordered social body.

Against this, the rise of Enlightenment thought heralded a belief in essential human equality, and saw rationality come to the fore, both as the defining characteristic of the human subject and as a central element in the constitution of society. The adoption of scientific reasoning to explain the ordering of the social necessitated a break with the forces of tradition and authority. As Scheman argues for the human subject, 'the cost of making that break was a concurrent break with the subject's own body, a break that was characterised and experienced as fundamental to individual empowerment' (1993:187). The emancipatory project of the Enlightenment, to liberate man [sic] from superstition and unreason and to ensure the autonomy of the rational ego, depended upon his freeing his thinking self from the ties of the body. And in privileging the mind over the body, 'it became impossible to empower the mind without disempowering or stigmatising the body' (1993:95).

What must be stressed is that not all minds were valued equally or all bodies held to be equally contaminating and dangerous to the rational ego. The supposedly universal subject was gendered male, for whilst both men and women have material bodies, it was the healthy male body that was taken to interfere least with transcendence. A necessary vehicle to house the soul and mind, such a body could be taken for granted, could rest unacknowledged, as long as emotion or illness did not cause it to disrupt thought.

In contrast, women were held to be intrinsically unable to separate themselves from their physical ties. The new philosophical thinking both constituted women as essentially embodied, thus excluding them from the realm of transcendent sub-jecthood, and simultaneously (through its identification of men with the privileged term in a series of hierarchical dualisms), served to reinforce women's pre-existing social disadvantages. The irony of this was that whilst women were viewed as inferior, by reason of their bodies, the possibility of emancipation, of empower-ment, was denied to them precisely because they were unable to break with these same bodies. And this exclusion holds not simply for women but for all those whose bodies fail to meet the 'mythical norm' Lorde (1984:116) in a diversity of ways: disabled people (Shakespeare 1994); those living with illness; black people and people of colour (Trepagnier 1994); gay men and lesbians (Corbett 1994). Identified as 'body', as Nature, defined as Other within the rationale of the economy of the Same, they are excluded not only from the position of ideal knower but also from any possibility of holding power, of being 'empowered'.

The move to identify who is to count as the same, who as different has served not only as a mechanism to exclude those who do not fit the norm but also, converse-ly, as a rallying point for a politics of identity widely adopted in the 1970s and 1980s by those who are marginalised in society. Central to the concept of identity politics has been an assertion of 'common experiences' that serve to unite groups of those similarly oppressed, such as women, lesbians and gay men, or disabled people. The development of social constructionist theories has offered an analysis of the oppression and disempowerment of certain groups on the basis of' for example, the social constitution of race and/or gender and/or sexuality. Theorising has explicitly rejected an appeal to a biological body, for such an appeal was seen to risk essentialising and thus 'naturalising' oppression. In consequence, the body/our bodies are at risk of being split off and silenced. As Lois McNay (1992:22) has argued, in relation to sexual difference and the sex/gender dichotomy, 'by privileging the gender side of this equation, the body is in effect neutralized and denied any salience whatsoever'. And yet the history of identity categories suggests that the body has played (and continues to play) a central role in their formation The late nineteenth and early twentieth centuries were a period during which biologism held strong sway, and hereditary explanations were put forward to explain differences between groups within society men and women, most obviously – but they were also used to explain the inferiority of colonised peoples, of homosexuals, of the poor, of disabled people (Mort 1987). These biological or hereditary explanations of the early twentieth century produced categories that were similar to those around which oppressed groups have organised themselves in more recent history. As Donna Haraway (1989:13) has highlighted, a competing network of discourses has been brought into play around the body: 'The marked organic body has been a critical locus of cultural and political contestation, crucial both to the languages of liberatory politics of identity and to systems of domination drawing on widely shared languages of nature constructed as resource for the appropriation of culture'.

Yet the binary logic of identity, by which any identity is always 'dependent on what is exterior to it' (Fuss 1991: 4), 'ablebodiedness'[2] on disability, heterosexuality on homosexuality, the healthy on the ill, applies likewise to the theoretical underpinnings of identity. The social constructionist arguments advocated in an identity politics of the 1980s and 1990s were set up in opposition to the regulatory biological categories of the 1920s, and they cannot be totally divorced from each other. It is the unmarked or privileged terms in such binaries – white, healthy, heterosexual – that hold the power of the 'natural'[3], the unconstructed, against which the constructions of a disabled or gay identity are posed. Furthermore, social con-structionism has not brought the biological body into question, but rather lain a constructed view of the world over it. Informing many of the identity categories currently in play today is an appeal to the body as hidden referent, grounding ontological status both historically and experientially.[4]

What I want to look to are some of those radical political movements that have, in various ways, addressed bodies and their differing materialisations, to highlight the implications of the preceding critique of bodies and empowerment for the emancipatory politics they have espoused, and to differing conceptions of power, knowledge and bodies that may offer us new possibilities for strategic political action.

The Women's Health Movement

The women's health movement grew around an explicitly political agenda that drew upon the early days of the women's movement, in its commitment to consciousness raising and to women gaining knowledge and challenging institutional structures that influence health. Women's bodies are central to the whole purpose of the women's health movement, and one of the foci was to try to clarify the relationship between the body as biology and the body as socially constructed. In contesting the belief that women were their bodies – that biology was destiny – a notion of a pre-given, biological, sexed body which was mediated by social processes came into play. Political activity was directed towards challenging the varying pathological constructions of the female body and the conception that women were inherently sick, and to opposing male-dominated medical control in areas such as childbirth. A central element in the growth of political activism in women's health was the exchange of experience, ideas and knowledge between women. Feminist self-help groups were an early feature of the women's movement and there continue to be many active today. *Our Bodies, Ourselves*, a major influence on women's health/movement, explains that self-help is 'political because it challenges health-care providers and gives us more control over our bodies' (Phillips and Rakusen 1989:639).

Women are to achieve freedom by knowing our bodies, emancipation from oppression and from pathologisation by the medical profession by gaining control over them. And many women have found in the women's health movement an enormous source of strength and support. Yet, as Wendi Hadd argues, 'The notion of being entitled to control one's body is formulated within a discourse which accepts as a given the concept of mind/body dualism' (1991:165). The body is positioned as an object apart and the aim is to ensure that its 'owner' is the one who exerts control, challenging health care providers to relinquish their power over the female body. We again find ourselves caught in a binary, witness to both the ongoing struggle for control over the body that is held to take place between medical professionals and women, and to the struggle that divides woman from her body. As Val Walsh (1995:6) argues, ' "having control" and "being human" are very closely connected' . . . 'evidence of wear and tear signifies loss of control accompanied by loss of human status'. The out-of-control is the deviant, that which cannot be contained within fixed boundaries, the less-than-human – and it is our bodies (through illness or impairment, and notably through being female – the potential for menstruation and conception) which repeatedly are held to signify this disruption and to disqualify us from humanity. Within this framework, women (and other Others) cannot exist as fully embodied subjects – for either we follow a route to empowerment and autonomy that demands we separate ourselves from our bodies in order to control them, or we remain tied to them, disempowered by our very identification with them.

The Disabled People's Movement

Both the women's health movement and the disabled people's movement have challenged the notion of disabled people and women as essentially sick. In contrast to the women's health movement, however, the trend within disabled politics has been to focus not on bodies but on the social construction of disability. Writers such as Oliver (1990) have offered a materialist analysis of disability, arguing that it is not the fact of impairment, i.e. 'the functional limitations which affect a person's body' (Morris 1993:*x*), but the social construction of disability that oppresses disabled people. A critique of medicalisation has developed that has similarities to the feminist critique in addressing the way in which the individual has been pathologised for failing to meet an unspoken norm – in this case, that of ablebodiedness. Disabled activists have located the discrimination and prejudice faced by disabled people as lying not in bodies that have 'traditionally been cast as aberrant markers of inherent inferiority and personal misfortune' (Thomson 1994:584) but in attitudes and exclusionary practices that are institutionalised in the fabric of society (Barnes and Oliver 1995:114). Thus, they argue for a shift in focus from the physical capability of an individual to a critique of the failure of society 'to adjust to the needs and aspirations of citizens with disabilities' (Barton 1993:237-8). This failure leads to prejudice and discrimination not only at a personal level, but has marked material and emotional consequences for disabled people; poverty, unemployment, loss of children, physical and sexual abuse (Begum 1992, Keith 1992, Morris 1993). In response, Barnes and Oliver (1995:115) suggest a programme of campaigns for civil rights legislation, and political action by disabled people which will include 'consciousness raising, direct action, the strengthening of democratic and accountable organisations, and the promotion and control of research'.

Within this set of proposals for action are combined the elements for a process of empowerment. Nira Yuval-Davis (1994:180), drawing on feminist writings, suggests empowerment can be perceived as:

> a process which breaks the boundaries between the public and the private domain, that comes out of the personal into the social and which connects the sense of the personal and the communal.

Her subsequent critique addresses how notions of empowerment have assumed a transition from personal to collective power, and have thus been closely linked to the concept of community. 'Community' has come to represent an entity which is naturalised and organic, internally homogeneous, and to which one either belongs or not, depending upon where the boundaries of the community are drawn. Referring to Homi Bhabha (1994:181), she argues:

> The 'naturalness' of the 'community' assumes a given collectivity with given boundaries – it allows for internal growth and probably differentia-tion but not for ideological and material reconstruction of the boundaries themselves.

A disability politics such as that advocated by Oliver and Barnes is predicated upon the notion of a disabled community becoming empowered, of individuals developing a collective awareness of the mechanisms of their oppression and ini-tiating joint action. Recent campaigns by disabled people's movements for a Disabled Rights Bill, for disabled people to be appointed as chief officers in charities previously *for* disabled people rather than run *by* them, and campaigns against the new incapacity benefit have all exemplified the growing strength and confidence of the disability movement. Alongside this has come a diversifica-tion, a widening of the boundaries to include, though not without contention, those with mental health problems, people with learning disabilities, and those with chronic illnesses such as HIV/AIDS and Myalgic Encephalomyelitis (ME) within the disabled community. This move has necessitated a rethink of both the material and ideological boundaries of disability politics and has brought to the fore troubling questions of identity, subjectivity, embodiment and representation.

The issue of who is to count as the same, as disabled, has become ever more complex. A liberal notion of difference, where the single binary opposition is mul-tiplied to take account of differences, as for example in an ever-increasing list of gender, race, class, age, sexuality, disability – or in the case of the disability movement, an ever extending list of qualifiers of disability – will not serve finally to distinguish those who are within and those who are outside the community.

Neither does an appeal to the body appear to provide any answers. Critiques of the medicalisation of disability argued that there could be no appeal to a 'natural' impaired body, but this rejection appears to have widened to a silencing of the discourse of bodies, marking a fear of being pulled back to a situation where disabled people are nothing but their bodies. As Jenny Morris (1991:10) has written, 'there is a tendency within the social model of disability to deny the expe-rience of our bodies, insisting that our physical differences and restrictions are entirely socially created'. The limitations of an appeal to such theories are revealed by the often unspoken hierarchies that exist within parts of the disabled people's movement between those born with impairments and those who acquire them in later life, those with 'permanent disabilities' and those with 'chronic illnesses' or 'invisible disabilities'. Whilst advocating a social model of disability, the body becomes the hidden arbiter of disabled status, producing an essentialist (biological)/constructionist tension at the very heart of disabled politics which threatens to undermine its radical project.

However, more recent work within the field of disability studies has returned to the body. Thomson suggests that it has drawn on aspects of identity politics to interrogate 'the prevailing interpretation of disability as corporeal inferiority, recasting it instead as another form of embodied difference which, like race and gender, has traditionally been interpreted as inadequacy' (1994:584). For example, a recent article by Tom Shakespeare (1994:283) touches upon the way in which the denial of the body has been part of a neglect of issues of culture, representation and meaning within disability writing. He develops an analysis of disabled people as Other, 'by virtue of their connection to nature; their visibility as evidence of the constraining body; and their status as constant reminders of mortality' and argues, in an inversion of the usual hierarchies associated with the 'disabled body', and it is not us, it is non-disabled people's embodiment which is the issue: disabled people remind non-disabled people of their own vulnerability' (1994:297). This questioning of the accepted hierarchy between non-disabled and disabled (in which disabled people are the marked term, 'the issue'), the recognition of the need to problematise non-disabled people, lays the ground both for a thoroughgoing deconstruction of fixed identities and for a notion of embodiment in which the boundaries of the body as well as the subject can be regarded as unstable and provisional. Jackie Stacey (1995) suggests that the mistake is to treat body margins as separate from other margins, to assume that they are fixed, certain, predetermined by a foundational biology . Viewed in this way, 'the physical impairments underlying disability are no longer seen as essential biological characteristics of a "real" body, upon which disability as a social construction is then imposed. Rather, they are themselves constructs held in place by the regulatory practices that both produce and govern bodies' (Price and Shildrick 1994:4).

Beyond identity politics?
What the above critique would suggest is the need to rethink not only the notions of identity and subjectivity but also notions of power and of the body and to look again at how they are related to each other, and how they might inform our politics. For whilst some might read the above critique of the subject and identity as destroying the grounds for many political movements, I would suggest that it offers us not an end to politics but a revaluation of the basis of our political projects. As Pragna Patel (1995) argues, there is a 'need to move beyond identity

politics, which paralysed us from reaching out to each other'. We need to look for a theorisation of power that offers us a route out of the eternal juggling act, the constant shuttling to and fro between those who have power and those who do not. We need not simply to account for the material effects of power, but propose ways in which our diverse materialisations – as subjects – as female – as disabled – as black – are not seen as reasons for excluding us from the realm of power. Thus, I would argue we need both a new notion of power and a different understanding of how we are constituted as embodied subjects.

Foucault argues that from the seventeenth century, power has evolved not in the repressive, top-down form manifest through politico-economic relations (1980:89) as proposed by a liberal or Marxist theorisation, but rather as a productive force, 'that is exercised from innumerable points' (1978:94), a network between whose threads people circulate, 'simultaneously undergoing and exercising this power' (1980:98). The body is indispensable to power – 'nothing is more material, physical, corporal than the exercise of power' (1980:57-8) – but the bodies of which Foucault speaks are neither 'natural' biological bodies nor social construc- tions of the corpus. Rather they are both the object and effect of discourse, produced and normalised through a network of relations of power which extend throughout the social body. They are material but always already constructed.

Whilst Foucault viewed relations of force as operating not in a vacuum or through abstract discursive forms but through embodied subjects, other postmodern thinkers, in critiquing the universal and essential (body) have appealed rather to a body that is fractured and dispersed, with shifting boundaries and a loss of the sense of the material – of the 'experiences'/facts of illness, disability and old age (Potts and Price 1995). There has been a denial not simply of the material effects of the exercise of power, but that power relations are exercised through embodied subjects, who are marked by gender, race, disability: that such relations are neces- sarily corporeal. Feminist writers such as Judith Butler (1993:10) have argued that the body is constructed by discourse, that 'there is no reference to a pure body which is not at the same time a further formation of that body'. She thus 'lays the ground for a material body which is not a natural body, for embodied subjectivity which is both the object and effect of discourse' (Potts and Price 1995:111).

At an individual level, how we are embodied is unstable, it is 'not something reliably constant' (Riley 1988:106). Although I can provide a neat list of categories to position myself, what these mean changes continuously, different aspects hold greater weight in different situations. For someone such as myself, with ME, and who is white, lesbian and middle class 'being a woman' will mean something entirely different from someone born with a visible impairment, or who is a single mother or who may be working class or black or straight or . . . The meaning I give to being a disabled woman and a lesbian varies: on the club scene, access problems exclude me from many venues and, even if I do get in, the cult of the body beautiful marks me as not a 'real' lesbian; using a wheelchair to shop around town, my sexuality is denied and my lover is seen as my 'carer'; on Pride, my sexuality and disability seem to have lined up together – until I am confronted by a flight of steps at the station blocking my way to the party in the park.

My subjectivity is provisional, my awareness of my own embodiment variable, and my sense of my self continually disrupted as Foucault (1984:87-8) says, 'nothing in man – not even his body – is sufficiently stable to serve as the basis for self-recognition or for understanding other men'. Although Foucault could be read as using man in the generic sense, his conflating of humanity with maleness reveals more vividly how, if the male body, the referent standard, cannot offer a stable sense of self, of identity, how much less feasible this task will be for those whose bodies are the mark of their Otherness. If our self-identity is provisional and unstable, identity politics breaks down, for it is not possible to identify a fixed unifying factor, whether material or discursive, that brings such an apparently disparate group together within, for example, the disabled people's or women's health movement. It is not just, as I suggested earlier, that the maintenance of identity always depends on an exterior, defined as lack, which becomes increasingly difficult to identify as the grounds of identity become ever more diverse. As Fuss (1991:3) goes on to argue, it is that lack is a feature of the self. 'The self erects and defends its borders against an other which is made to represent that selfsame lack' . And the boundaries between sameness and difference, self and other are revealed as not only materially, but discursively, leaky and highly unstable and, as subject positions, purely provisional. In 'Breaking the Boundaries of the Broken Body', Margrit Shildrick and I write,

> In a reworking of the separation of self and other, there can be no under-
> standing of, for example, able-bodied, unless there is already an implicit
> distinction being made that to be able-bodied is not to be disabled. Yet
> because able-bodied carries within it the trace of the other – a trace which
> must be continually suppressed if able-bodied is to carry a delimited
> meaning – such closure is not possible. To deconstruct binary difference
> then, to point up all those oppositional categories which begin to undo
> themselves at the very moment of defining identity through exclusion,

disrupts both ontological and corporeal security. In other words, the spectre of the other always already haunts the selfsame: it is the empty wheelchair that generates disease in the fully mobile.(Price and Shildrick 1994:12)

Identity formation takes place against the other, the outside, lack – but this policing of identity boundaries does not only take place by those traditionally viewed as being on the inside – white people, non-disabled people, heterosexual – but also by the outsiders, the marginalised. This is not to argue that non-disabled and disabled people occupy positions of mutual interchangeability, of equivalent power deriving from the process of identity formation, for power does not flow equally between centre and the margins. Rather, it is that the centre and margins are not fixed and that in policing their own identity, disabled people identify non-disabled people as the outside, and have to constantly struggle to maintain the boundaries that mark the site of their difference.

As Fuss (1991:5) suggests, however, there is a further problem 'with the inside/outside rhetoric, if it remains undeconstructed (which) is that such polemics disguise the fact that most of us are both inside and outside at the same time'. To claim identity, any identity, is to place oneself in a relative position of insiderhood: it is to find a voice, to move from a position of speechlessness and powerlessness (Fuss 1991). But such insiderhood is always unstable, for there is no single centre lined up against a permanent outside, but rather multiple and shifting ins and outs. Within gay politics, one strategy adopted by some campaigning groups has been to 'out' gay men and lesbians who are public figures and who have refused to identify themselves as gay. Whatever the various rationales used to advocate such 'outings', they are predicated upon the notion that through the assignation of the sign 'gay', it will become clear exactly what that person is, that their identity will be revealed. Interestingly, disability activists are advocating a similar process of 'outing' for those people identified by the movement as disabled, but who refuse to claim that identity for themselves (London Disability News 1995:5).

As Butler argues:

in the act which would disclose the true and full content of that "I", a certain radical concealment is thereby produced. For it is always finally unclear what is meant by invoking the lesbian (*or disabled/black/woman*) signifier, since its signification is always to some degree out of one's control, but also because its specificity can only be demarcated by exclusions that return to disrupt its claim to coherence (Butler 1991:1 5). (My addition in italics.)

To return to the disability movement, (and to paraphrase Butler), 'what, if anything, can *disabled people* be said to share? And who will decide this question, and in the name of whom?'(1991: 15). In raising these questions, my aim is not to deny the importance of the women's health and disabled people's movement, but to address the implications of notions of empowerment for a view of women and disabled people as embodied subjects, whose diversity is recognised.

Donna Haraway (1988.594-5) offers a possible analysis that brings together bodies, knowledge and power. Bodies are not simply objects, constituted by discourse from the outside, or a resource to be managed to gain maximum utility, but are agents, playing a part in mapping their own boundaries. She draws on standpoint theories[5] and, on post structuralism/deconstruction to argue for a politics of location, of situated and embodied knowledges, where the partial 'view from somewhere' is deemed to have more credibility than the relativist view from everywhere or the transcendent, objectifying view from nowhere. Her vision is of 'partial, locatable, critical knowledges sustaining the possibility of webs of connections called solidarity in politics and shared conversations in epistemology' (1988:584). What she proposes allows no easy answers for subjugated groups. There can be no ready appeal to a common identity, to the authority of experience, even to the body (whether given or constructed) as the basis for knowledge claims or political action.

But, Haraway (1988:585) argues, if totalising identities are problematic, neither will just any partial perspective serve: she warns of the need to be wary of 'easy relativisms and holisms built out of summing and subsuming parts'. For example, within parts of the women's health or disability movements, the perceived need to present a readily comprehensible and unified political programme risks silencing voices of diversity and may try to force a unity between groups where needs and aspirations differ widely. She proposes the need for a commitment to 'mobile positioning and to passionate detachment' (1988:585).

Conclusion
In writing about the politics of the women's health and disability movements, in attempting to theorise empowerment and the body, I am constantly aware of my partial location, of all the voices I have not heard or read, or having read, have not found ways of including their other and often counterdiscursive views, into my writing. I worry that in trying to present an argument, I have silenced the very diversity for which I am making a plea. And I wonder about the voices within myself which I may have silenced because they do not seem to fit.

Eve Kosofsky Sedgwick (1993:12) turned to deconstruction when she had breast cancer – with similar concerns about ' "applying" theoretical models to particular situations or texts' – and suggests that she found it 'can offer crucial resources of thought for survival under duress'. It allows one to hold on to experience without essentialising it, to recognise difference without reifying it, to act at strategic moments without the necessity for a totalising answer. Spivak (1993:4) argues, 'the most serious critique in deconstruction is the critique of things that are extremely useful, things without which we cannot live on, take chances; like our running self-identikit'

For both Eve Sedgwick and Audre Lorde, in the face of a life-threatening illness, the acknowledgement of difference, albeit in quite distinct ways, became a focus of their experience of breast cancer. Sedgwick (1993:13) speaks of 'hurling my energies outward to inhabit the very farthest of the loose ends where representation, identity, gender, sexuality and the body can't be made to line up neatly together', whilst Lorde (1988:117-8) said, 'I have always known I learn my most lasting lessons about difference by closely attending the ways in which the differences inside me lie down together'.

As I think of differences, of the possibilities of resistance, subversion, disruption of boundaries, I am brought up against the material effects of ill health and disability, as they operate, for example, through the disciplinary regime of the new incapacity benefit (IB). Through this benefit, illness is reconstituted in relation to the economic; new norms of health and illness, non-disabled and disabled, are established. The spectre of wheelchairs causes disease in the fully mobile, yet this time the wheelchairs are not empty but occupied by 'wheelchair "fraudsters" ' (White 1995); people who, in the words of Peter Lilley, Social Security Secretary, 'have been refused benefit and, for the first time in their lives, they will be seen in a wheelchair' (White 1995). In the face of such an exercise of power/knowledge, with the added potential of financial gain or loss, deconstruction may seem an empty ploy and, as Tracey Potts (1995) says, one 'wants meaning to behave itself'.

Thus, in advocating the strengths of a deconstructive approach to power and the embodied subject, in reflecting on how this alters understandings of illness and disability, for example, I need to be aware that a new binary is established, that of undecidability and fixity, in which the former occupies the privileged epistemological site. The transgressive move, the exercise of resistance, may in some cases be the disruption of accepted meaning whilst in others, the claim to fixity or certainty can prove to be a valuable strategy for survival. The danger lies in one or the other becoming the only strategy available to us – either of identity which cannot/will not be disrupted or of the subject forever in flux.

Our differences are a resource, not a problem to be overcome. Our strength lies in not closing things down; in moving beyond simply acknowledging difference to doing something with it (plenary discussion at WSN 1995 Conference).

Notes
[1] Phenomenological notions of the body regard the healthy body as the unbroken body, paradoxically absent in the state of health for it does not draw attention to itself. It is only when this state of wholeness is broken, by illness, disability and significantly the changes of the female body through menstruation and pregnancy – that the body comes into awareness, forcing itself on the attention of the subject, experienced as 'broken', as other (Shildrick 1995).

[2] Within the social model of disability, the term non-disabled people is preferred to able-bodied people because 'people who do not experience physical, sensory or intellectual impairment are not disabled by the prejudice and discrimination which denies opportunities to people who experience such impairments' (Morris 1993:x) At times, I use the term abled-bodied to draw attention to the need to deconstruct it as the unmarked term in the disabled/abled bodied binary.

[3] The use of 'natural' here expresses its contradictory use in general. 'On the one hand it is valorised as the site of the proposer, of the pure and uncontaminated. . .' of the white, heterosexual male; and on the other, 'when set against culture, nature is at best base and unruly - that which must be controlled' (Shildrick 1995: 2). It is the body, women, disabled people's other Others.

[4] This referent body has recently re-emerged and taken a more prominent place in debates around identity. See for example the work of Simon Le Vay (1992) on differences in brain structure between gay and straight men, and its adoption by some as providing a biological explanation of sexuality.

[5] See Haraway (1988) and Collins (1990) for further discussion of standpoint theory

References
Barnes, C. and Oliver, M. (1995) 'Disability Rights: rhetoric and reality in the UK' in *Disability and Society* 10,1,111-116

Barton, L. (1993) 'The Struggle for Citizenship: the case of disabled people' in *Disability, Handicap and Society*, 8, 3,235-248.

Begum, N. (1992) 'Disabled Women and the Feminist Agenda' in *Feminist Review*, 40, 70-84.

Butler, J. (1991) 'Imitation and Gender Insubordination' in Fuss, D. (Ed.) *inside/out. Lesbian Theories, Gay Theories*. New York and London: Routledge.

Butler, J. (1993) *Bodies That Matter: On the Discursive Limits of "Sex"*. New York and London: Routledge.

Collins, P. H. (1990) *Black Feminist Thought, Knowledge, Consciousness, and the Politics of Empowerment*. New York and London: Routledge.

Corbett, J. (1994) 'A Proud Label: exploring the relationship between disability politics and gay pride' in *Disability and Society*, 9, 3, 343-357.

Foucault, M. (1978) *The History of Sexuality, Volume 1: An Introduction*. Harmondsworth: Penguin Books Ltd.

Foucault, M. (1980) *Power/Knowledge: Selected Interviews and Other Writings, 1972-77*. C. Gordon (Ed.) Brighton: The Harvester Press Ltd.

Foucault, M. (1984) 'Nietzsche, genealogy, history' in Rabinow, P. (Ed.) *The Foucault Reader*. Harmondsworth: Penguin Books Ltd.

Fuss, D. (Ed) (1991) *inside/out. Lesbian Theories, Gay Theories*. New York and London: Routledge.

Gatens, M. (1992) 'Power, Bodies and Difference', in Barrett, M. and Phillips, A. (Eds.) *Destabilizing Theory, Contemporary Feminist Debates*. Cambridge: Polity Press.

Hadd, W. (1991) 'A Womb with A View: Women as Mothers and the Discourse of the Body' in *Berkeley Journal of Sociology*; 36, 165-175.

Haraway, D. (1988) 'Situated Knowledges: The Science Question in Feminism and the Privilege of Partial Perspective' in *Feminist Studies*, 14,3,575-599.

Haraway, D. (1989) 'The Biopolitics of Postmodern Bodies: Determinations of Self in Immune System Discourse' in *Differences*, 1,1,3-43.

Keith, L. (1992) 'Who Cares Wins? Women, Caring and Disability' in *Disability, Handicap and Society*, 7,2, 167-175.

Lather, P. (1991) *Getting Smart: Feminist Research and Pedagogy With/In the Postmodern*. New York and London: Routledge.

LeVay, S. (1992) 'Are homosexuals born and not made?' in *The Guardian*, 9 October 1992, 31.

London Disability News (1995) 'Dead or Alive' in Commentary, May, 5.

Lorde, A. (1984) *Sister Outsider*. New York: The Crossing Press.

Lorde, A. (1988) *A Burst of Light*. London: Sheba Feminist Publishers.

McNay, L. (1992) Foucault and Feminism. Cambridge: Polity Press.

Morris, J. (1991) *Pride Against Prejudice*. Transforming Attitudes to Disability. London: The Women's Press.

Morris, J. (1993) *Independent Lives*. London: The MacMillan Press Ltd.

Morris, J. (1993) 'Feminism and Disability' in Feminist Review, 43,57-70.

Mort, F. (1987) *Dangerous Sexualities. Medico-moral politics in England since 1830*. London and New York: Routledge and Kegan Paul.

Oliver, M. (1990) *The Politics of Disablement*. London: The MacMillan Press Ltd.

Patel, P. (1995) Plenary Paper presented at the WSN (UK) Conference, Stirling University, June 1995.

Phillips, A. and Rakusen, J. (Eds.) (1989) *The New Our Bodies, Ourselves,* Boston Women's Health Collective. Harmondsworth: Penguin Books Ltd.

Potts, T. (1995) *"Adventures in Applied Deconstruction": Queering Illness*. Paper presented at 'Queer Bodies' Conference, Warwick University, May 1995.

Potts, T. and Price, J. (1995) ' "Out of the Blood and Spirit of Our Lives": The Place of the Body in Academic Feminism' in Morley, L. and Walsh, V. (Eds) *Feminist Academics: Creative Agents for Change*. London: Taylor and Francis.

Price, J. and Shildrick, M. (1994) *Breaking the Boundaries of the Broken Body*. Paper presented at WSN (UK) Conference, Portsmouth University, July 1994.

Riley, D. (1988) *'Am I That Name?' Feminism and the Category of 'Woman' in History*. London: The MacMillan Press Ltd.

Scheman, N. (1993) E*ngenderings. Constructions of Knowledge, Authority, and Privilege*. New York and London: Routledge. Sedgwick, E. K. (1993) Tendencies. Durham: Duke University Press.

Shakespeare, T. (1994) 'Cultural Representation of Disabled People: dustbins for disavowal?' in *Disability and Society*, 9,3, 283-299.

Shildrick, M. (1995) *Posthumanism and the Monstrous Body:* Paper presented at 'Beyond Antihumanism' Conference, University of Manchester, May 1995.

Spivak, G. (1993) *Outside in the Teaching Machine.* New York and London: Routledge.

Stacey, J. (1995) *The C word and the L word*: Cultural Taboo and Abjection. Paper presented at 'Queer Bodies' Conference, Warwick University, May 1995.

Thomson, R. G. (1994) 'Redrawing the Boundaries of Feminist Disability Studies' in *Feminist Studies*, 20, 3, 583-595.

Trepagnier, B. (1994) 'The Politics of White and Black Bodies' in Bhavnani, K. and Phoenix, A. (Eds.) *Shifting Identities Shifting Racisms*. London: Sage Publications Ltd.

Walsh, V. (1995) 'Disability Feminism'. Draft of conceptual entry in Kramarae, C. and Spender, D. (Eds.) *Women's Studies Encyclopaedia.* (Forthcoming).

White, M. (1995) 'Lilley on alert for wheelchair "fraudsters" in new benefit tests' in *The Guardian* 4 May 1995, 8

Yuval-Davis, N. (1994) 'Women, Ethnicity and Empowerment' in Bhavnani, K. and Phoenix A. (Eds.) *Shifting Identities Shifting Racisms*. London: Sage Publications Ltd.

Chapter 4
'Carers' and 'Caring': New Thoughts on Old Questions

Barbara Fawcett and Brid Featherstone

Introduction

'Carers' and 'caring' are words which would currently appear to be drowning in rhetoric. Intensely contested, they apply to both public and private spheres and to the interface between. In this chapter we explore current debates and engage with feminist explorations of poststructuralism and postmodernism to assess their relevance and applicability to 'carers', 'caring' and social work.

'Carers' and 'Caring': Consumerism and Empowerment

Any review of 'Carers' and 'caring' must explore and be located within current discussions around consumerism, consultation and empowerment. The White Paper 'Caring for People'(1989) which informed the NHS and Community Care Act (1990) asserted that the changes outlined were intended to 'give people a greater individual say in how they live their lives and the services they need to help them to do so'(1990:1.8:4). However, whilst consumer choice may seem like a 'good thing', it is questionable whether needs and services in areas such as health and welfare can be commodified and made accessible to individuals in a 'catalogue' fashion. Resource issues provide one area of difficulty, as do tensions between professionally assessed need and self-assessed need (Fawcett and Featherstone 1994). There are also contradictions in consumer rhetoric which focuses on individuals making choices and purchases in a mixed-economy-of care supermarket, whilst disregarding the fact that it is a third party (i.e. social services) who actually purchase services on behalf of individuals, to meet agency-assessed needs. Similarly, different needs and different choices tend to be conflated, with the market being heralded as the place where both find expression and where conflicts are miraculously resolved (Williams 1995).

Dissatisfaction with consumerist interpretations has led to an increased use of the term 'empowerment'. This has come to mean different things to different people. Writers such as Solomon (1976), Croft and Beresford (1990), Beresford and Croft (1993), Braye and Preston-Shoot (1993), Ward and Mullender (1992) have conceptualised empowerment in a variety of ways and all have included associated practical guidelines for its successful delivery. However, whilst Beresford and Croft (1993) and Bray and Preston-Shoot (1993) highlight the complexities involved, others tend to regard empowerment and empowering strategies as straight forwardly positive and necessary. We question this assumption and whilst we would not want to dismiss empowerment as a process which in certain sets of circumstances can have considerable practical utility, we draw attention to the complexities involved. Baistow (1995), for example, emphasises that empowerment has both regulatory and liberatory possibilities which are not simply or straightforwardly tied to the individual motivations of those involved. She draws attention to the possible negative consequences for service users of empowerment being used to justify professional positions and interventions and being incorporated within job descriptions on a routinised basis. Similarly, Dowson (1990) highlights how the term may be used to legitimise all kinds of activities which may not be in the interests of service users. We argue therefore that in debates surrounding 'Carers' and 'caring', empowerment is a concept to use with caution.

Carers and Caring: A Review of Current Debates
Currently the role of carers and consideration of caring activities would appear to be high on the political agenda. The recent estimates of cash saved to the Government by domestic caring arrangements undoubtedly plays a part in this. Support for carers was highlighted in the White Paper 'Caring for People'(1989) which informed the NHS and Community Care Act (1990) and action is currently being taken with regard to legislation for carers. The Government has also demonstrated its 'commitment' by establishing carer forums which, by and large, bypass both local authority frameworks and independent user group arrangements, to report directly to the Department of Health. In addition, Community Care has spawned complex administrative structures within social services departments which affect most areas of social work including carers and caring activities.

The extent to which political and professional debates on caring reflect the views, wishes or needs of those at the receiving end of policies, remains contentious. Similarly, the level to which contested meanings and agendas in the public domain resonate in individual households struggling with roles, relationships, tasks and finances is an under-researched area. However, it is important to note that boundaries between public and private domains are not fixed and that there is fluidity at the interface. The extent, for example, to which women from particular classes and 'races' undertake the majority of hands-on tasks, whether it is in the NHS or as home care workers employed by social services departments or in the family home, means that it is important not to posit clear-cut distinctions.

Overall, it has to be acknowledged that the literature on 'carers' and 'caring' constitutes a rapidly expanding area (Pahl 1992). It is also apparent that within the literature, particular themes or groups or priorities tend to be focused on differentially. We shall now explore some of these areas in more detail and consider their significance.

Twigg and Atkin (1994) spotlight the carer and his/her relationship to the 'cared for' and the impact on this relationship of policy and practice. They provide useful insights into an area where 'there is little in the way of an established tradition about appropriate support for carers'(1994:29). They highlight the ambiguous position of carers and delineate four ways in which they can be regarded by professionals and agencies. These are as 'resources', 'co-workers', 'co-clients' and as 'superseded' carers. These varying roles carry differing implications in terms of how much support is offered and whose interests are judged to be paramount. They acknowledge power differentials but particularly draw attention to negotiation as a critical factor in the interaction between professional and carer.

Writers such as Finkelstein (1993), Morris (1993) and Oliver (1990; 1992; 1993) contest the use of a term such as 'cared for', highlighting its association with notions of dependency and lack of autonomy. Finkelstein and Oliver in particular emphasise the disabling barriers contained in medical, welfare and stereotypical models of 'care' and argue for the development of legislative and environmental policies which address and counteract disablism and paternalism. This challenge is taken up at the political level by organisations such as the British Council of Organisations of Disabled People, the Spinal Injuries Association, and the Disability Action Network.

With regard to feminism(s), from the late seventies attention has focused on the caring responsibilities carried by women and on deconstructing and unpacking the notion of 'caring' itself (Pahl 1992). Finch and Groves (1983) are generally accepted as providing the first analysis in this country. Their argument that care in the community equalled care by women was and to some extent continues to be widely accepted by feminists. Dalley (1988), for example, emphasises the role of the family in sanctioning, reinforcing and reproducing patterns of patriarchal relations which focus upon women's role as carers and family servicers. As an alternative she has promoted collectivist solutions for those requiring physical support. These views are increasingly contested by disabled feminist writers such as Morris (1993). She questions whether women can be viewed as a unitary category and takes issue with the exclusion of women with disabilities and older women who may also 'care' from some of the feminist literature. Talking of Sheila Willis, who has multiple sclerosis, Morris says: 'A feminist for fifteen years, her role as a mother and her ability to run her own house were intensely important to her; to deny this would be a denial of her fundamental human rights and those of her daughter'(Morris 1993:161/2)

Assumptions that locate caring relationships exclusively within models of the nuclear family are also questioned by Graham (1993). She contests the view that it is an activity mainly carried out by younger women/daughters for older parents and argues for the importance of recognising gay and lesbian relationships for example, particularly with regard to AIDS. She also notes the struggles waged by black women to be able to care in situations where families are divided because of racism and immigration. She maintains 'women occupy different positions, both in terms of their access to and responsibilities for care with these positions linked to their experiences of disability and their place in the hierarchies of "race", class and sexuality'(Graham 1993: 28).

Other writers have concentrated on challenging the assumption that caring is the sole prerogative of women. Green (1988) in his study of informal carers based on an analysis of General Household Survey information, identified 2.5 million male carers and 3.5 million female carers. He noted that female carers were more likely to care full time for relatives and male carers were more likely to be the main carer for their spouse. A further GHS report published in 1992 estimated that in 1990 approximately 2.9 million of the 6.8 million carers identified were men. Qureshi and Walker (1988), using Green's work, describe a hierarchy of caring relationships based on the nuclear family, patriarchal relationships and family ties. They identify that a caring spouse was first choice, followed by daughters, and then other close relatives. Arber and Gilbert (1993) assessed responses to a section of the 1980 General Household Survey which asked people over sixty-five about their ability to carry out domestic and self-care tasks and also whether they received statutory health and welfare services. They found that only 8% of elderly people in need of daily support lived with a younger married couple. In these circumstances the prevailing assumption was that the woman would be the primary caret. They also found that such daughters received considerably less support than male or female unmarried carers.

The studies indicate that men cannot be dismissed from caring equations. They show that men tend to be represented equally when it comes to caring for a spouse and play a significant part in other relationships, although women still tend to assume more responsibility and spend more time on caring activities. Fisher (1994) in particular challenges assumptions about age and gender. He argues that to be relevant and positively perceived, caring services have to be based on nego-tiation rather than assumption and on partnership rather than professional domi-nance. He asserts that, for this to happen, 'prevailing views about gender and care, need also to be fundamentally re-examined'(Fisher 1994:676.)

To summarise at this point, we emphasise that words such as 'carer' and 'caring' cannot be regarded as having a single or unitary meaning or as referring to fixed positions. As with empowerment, the complexities have to be acknowledged.

Perspectives to Consider
We now move on to consider perspectives drawn from postmodernism and post-structuralism. We particularly focus on interpretations of such perspectives made by feminist writers and assess the relevancy of these orientations for debates in relation to 'carers' and 'caring'.

It can be asserted that there are parallels between developments in feminism(s) and postmodernism and poststructuralism. This can be seen in relation to the deconstruction of taken-for-granted assumptions and the rejection of white Western male notions of knowledge and language frameworks as objective and value free. However there are divergences in that, initially, feminist re-appraisals of 'objective facts' were mounted on the basis of structural either/or analyses, where the unitary category 'woman' was repositioned, revalued and re-explored in relation to the unitary category 'man'. Experiential challenges by some femi-nists to such all-embracing views of 'women' which conversely focus on subject identities and essentialist notions of selfhood, also run counter to post-structural and postmodern orientations. Further points of overlap between feminism(s) and postmodernism and poststructuralism can be found in feminist critiques of the use of experience to validate fixed and essentialist positions and the consequent silencing of those who cannot claim to have experienced as many oppressions. Despite these similarities and divergences, the move by some feminists to actively explore poststructural and postmodern concepts was undoubtedly influenced by the view that such initially-male-dominated constructs were ignored at their peril. There was also the challenge of exploring what such perspectives may have to offer feminism(s).

With regard to postmodernism and poststructuralism[1], these are terms which, as Barrett (1992) asserts, should be employed with caution as they are used in a vari-ety of ways in many different contexts. Nevertheless, these conceptual frame-works can be seen as alerting us to some broad and important trends in current

thought of which writers such as Lacan, Derrida and Foucault are central expo-
nents. Barrett argues that these three writers signify what is a paradigm shift in
Western thought. Such a shift can be summed up in terms of a movement away
from things to words. Accordingly, analyses that explore meanings and language
and knowledge and power can be seen to he more influential than materialist
understandings.

Feminists who have explored postmodernist and poststructuralist perspectives
include Barrett (1992), Weedon (1987), Flax (1990:1992:1993), Sawicki (1991),
hooks (1991), Fraser and Nicholson (1993), and Williams (1992:1994:1995).
Whilst these writers do not offer a coherent and integrated analysis and indeed differ widely in many important respects, they all share a commitment to developing
understandings which are tentative and provisional. They are wary of stories
which assume the onward march of progress or that assert the possibility of objective, innocent knowledge. Attention has been focused, for example, on the
evidence from the twentieth century of the destructive as well as the emancipatory
possibilities of science. Similarly, various challenges are mounted to the modernist view of experience as a valid and transparent guide to truth and of the
human subject as comprising a privileged inner self with a defining essence.
Overall there is a move away from universal theories such as Marxism or liberal-
ism or certain versions of feminism which purport to explain and predict for all. A
concern to explore difference and context rather than universals and abstractions
is highlighted. There is also an emphasis on regarding differences as multiple and
shifting rather than as fixed or inevitable.

However, feminists who have explored postmodernist and poststructuralist concepts have highlighted problematic features. In particular, relativity, superficiality
and undifferentiated pluralism have proved difficult to reconcile with long-standing commitments to challenging inequality and social divisions. Accordingly,
many writers have sought to make links between feminism, post-structuralism
and postmodernism and construct pragmatic reformulations. bell hooks (1991) for
example, argues for a radical postmodernism which contains the possibility of
making links and constructing empathy and ties which could promote solidarity
and coalition building. Fraser and Nicholson (1993) critique many aspects of
modernism, such as universalism and notions of 'truth', rationality and objective
determinism. They see much in postmodern orientations which Is positive for
feminism but reject dalliance with notions of relativity. They maintain that feminism has come too far to dismiss social divisions and inequalities entirely. This
leads, as Barrett (1991) suggests, to a thorny theoretical problem where what is

sought is a means of avoiding universalistic pretensions without surrendering totally to particularism and relativism. Williams (1994) taking up the challenge, argues that debates concerning the shift in emphasis from things to words need not be viewed in either/or terms. She asserts: 'Rather the shift can be seen to provide the possibility of a more complex inquiry into the relationship between identity, agency, and welfare discourses, and how these combine in different ways to shape the materiality of people's lives'(Williams 1994:14 and 15).

Fraser and Nicholson maintain that analyses of societal macrostructures and large historical narratives are not inconsistent with postmodern theory. However, they stress that such theory must be historically reframed so that it is temporally and culturally specific and comparative rather than universalist. Incorporated within such a perspective would be the rejection of the idea of a subject of history and the replacement of a unitary notion of 'woman' and 'feminine gender identity' by plural and complexly constructed conceptions of social identity. They assert that 'this theory would look more like a tapestry composed of threads of many different hues than one woven in a single colour' (Fraser and Nicholson 1993).

Flax (1990, 1992 and 1993) has also noted both the dangers and the possibilities of postmodern discourses. She questions practices which in simply naming the marginalised perpetuate and legitimise discourses which continues to locate them at the margins. She recognises that some versions of postmodernism make it difficult to discuss questions of freedom, justice or equality at all. Flax also takes issue with the pragmatic politics advocated by Rorty and asks whether it leads to a politics where the person who shouts loudest will be the only one who is heard. She does, however, accept the concerns expressed by postmodernists about universalist schemata which are tyrannical in their homogeneity. She accepts Foucault's strictures about the relationship between power and knowledge and his understanding that oppositional forms of knowledge often extend the forms of domination they are contesting.

Flax, in her attempt to explore how a concern for difference and context can be rescued from sliding into a relativism which is unconcerned with or has no tools for understanding and countering domination, advances the notion of justice as a bridging concept. She views the concept of justice as having roots in classical theory where, unlike liberal theory, there was a recognition that people differed. She cautions against any search for universalist groundings for justice and for a recognition that the conditions and contexts in which it can flourish must be delimited.

Accordingly, it is not a set of finite rules instituted once and for all; rather it is an ongoing process where ideas of what is needed will change over time. She argues that it could be part of a process which enables the reconciliation of differences between self and other without domination and that it could teach us how to differ from the other without feeling a need to annihilate him or her.

> 'Understood as a process, justice is one way the individual manages the strain of being simultaneously public and private, alone and in relation to others, desiring and interdependent. On a collective level justice is one way groups manage the strain of mediating between the individual subjectivities of which they are composed and the objectivities such as limited resources, past traditions and the consequences of past decisions and practices which those individuals did not create but to which they must respond. The management of such tensions necessarily involves the exercise of various forms of power . . . however, depending on how the tensions are managed, empowerment and relief may result' (Flax 1992:205).

It is salient that feminists engaging in postmodernist debates quickly identify both utilisable and problematic factors. They seek to make links and to ensure that pertinent issues related to social divisions and differences are reframed rather than rejected. We now move on to examine whether such perspectives can be helpfully applied to the discussions surrounding 'carers' and 'caring'.

The application of perspectives
drawn from feminism, postmodernism and poststructuralism

The utilisation of postmodern and poststructural perspectives enables us to acknowledge difference, diversity and context. The reformulation propounded by Fraser and Nicholson emphasises these areas whilst at the same time acknowledging the material circumstances in which people live. Accordingly, enduring social divisions such as poverty, class, age, gender and 'race' have a place. This makes it possible to explore with carers the details of their lives and the interrelationships which operate whilst maintaining a focus on poverty or inequality in the treatment of male and female carers.

In a similar fashion postmodern and poststructural perspectives reject liberal notions of universal rights (the infringement of which become oppressions) and the idea of power as a thing which is imposed by the powerful upon the powerless (Sawicki 1991). The emphasis on relativity and context renders solidarity and universal notions of rights obsolete. This can be problematic in terms of appeals to universal frameworks of carers rights, or indeed of women's rights. However, the notion of justice put forward by Flax can be seen as a way of moving away from universalistic concepts without losing sight of a means of weighting differences and aspirations and initiating action.

Fiona Williams (1995) drawing from Barrett (1987) and Brah (1992) focuses on an exploration of difference, a concept which she regards as central to and a means of making links between feminism, postmodernism and poststructuralism. Williams looks at difference in terms of diversity, difference and division. By diversity she refers to specific shared collective experience which is not necessarily associated with subordination or inequality, such as nationality, age or physical condition. Difference relates to a shared collective experience or identity which forms the basis for resistance against subordinate positioning. Division is used to refer to the translation of a shared experience into a form of domination, for example being white heterosexual or male. These are not fixed categories, and it is made clear that a number of responses are possible. Groups can, for example, freeze projected or self-imposed identities and associated power relations. Such responses can lead to the development of clear-cut fixed oppositional frameworks. Groups can also focus on processes of mediation and negotiation and operate in the political arena and elsewhere on the basis of negotiated and temporarily formed and frozen identities, created with particular challenges in mind. Williams advocates pragmatism and contingency and notes that fixed groupings and rigidly maintained differences can all too easily lead to all groups competing for the same shrinking resources or for groups to be played off against each other.

Accordingly in relation to 'carers' and 'caring', an individual could belong to a number of different groups at the same point in time and engage in temporary negotiation and the freezing of difference in a variety of ways. For example, it may be political to temporarily freeze differences between female carers of older people in both public and private locations to draw attention to and campaign for realistic pay and conditions. Differences could also be temporarily frozen in relation to carers and service users with regard to campaigns about the self assessment of need and the provision of budgets to be allocated and spent by individual carers or service users, combinations of both or collectives. Such groupings could further include professionals and service users, campaigning for more resources or for brokerage or advocacy models of care management which enable service users or carers to operate as their own brokers or advocates.

In relation to social work, Howe (1994) has argued that postmodernism has mounted an effective critique of practice and perspectives within social work which posit a particular malestream or eurocentric viewpoint as the norm and which seek to explain a wide range of human activities and interactions on the basis of a small number of theoretical perspectives which can be universally applied. He further acknowledges that the 'rejection of modernity's pursuit of universal standards of truth, beauty and justice profoundly disturbs social work's intellectual and practical make-up'. (Howe 1994:523)

This can be seen to have creative potential; it can also be regarded as disturbing and disruptive. One of the ways in which agencies and to some extent social workers have responded to the breakdown of their grand narratives is to focus on the reduction of uncertainty. Accordingly, there has been an emphasis on employing techniques and types of knowledge which seek to render tasks and roles 'safe, predictable, workable and reliable' (Howe 1994:527). Howe maintains that this has resulted in a focus on contracts, task completion and skills. Here individuals strive to achieve specific certainties by focusing on procedure, commodification, law, contracts and rationality. Parton (1994) similarly writes of the emergence of a new discourse' concerning management, monitoring, evaluation and assessment which claims to provide the mechanisms for holding things together and which in the process seems to be central in constituting the nature of contemporary social work itself'(Parton 1994:30).

This search for small certainties can result in rigidity and a search for prescriptive frameworks which can be applied in a generalised way. With regard to concepts of empowerment, such inflexibility can be seen in the insistence on certain ground rules which are regarded as necessary to reach a clear-cut goal which is transparently and manifestly emancipatory for all concerned (Ward and Mullender 1992). Similarly, the implications for 'care' and 'caring' are to seek standardised practices and procedures which can be applied in a routinised manner. This militates against the exploration of diversity and the ongoing negotiation of what is appropriate (Twigg and Atkin 1994: Fisher 1994). Further, as the literature indicates, we have moved away from universal stories. It is also likely that attempts to impose small certainties will prove counterproductive.

The perspectives outlined which draw from feminism, postmodernism and poststructuralism focus attention on the possibilities contained in work which is contextual, located and alert to contradiction. In relation to carers and caring activities, this emphasises the complexities, contradictions and changes often ignored or glossed over. Opie, for example, found, in her research into caregiving, evidence of contradictory and complex feelings of love, pain, distress and pride. She also discovered that:

'constituents were unstable and differently constituted by, for example, generational positioning, age, gender, ideology, prior experience of acting as care giver, the past and current relationship with the elderly person and the ability to command resources'(Opie 1992:55).

Opie further observed that in the space of a few minutes the expressed view of a carer could change from frustration, to hope, to anger, to love and that a mix of emotions could be held simultaneously. This can be contrasted to professional expectations about accepted behaviour and to assumptions that individuals should behave rationally, coherently and give accounts in a linear and consistent way. Less-rigid and fixed operational expectations can lead to the questioning of attitudes adopted towards those who are not seen to perform in the expected manner and a greater recognition of the complexity of factors and value judgements involved. Flax's work (1992) also enables us to explore understandings in relation to power/knowledge frameworks and to review the possibilities of work which takes a less 'innocent' view of existing structures and activities. This facilitates the questioning of taken-for-granted assumptions and prescriptive formulations. It further provides space for a wide range of orientations and for negotiations to take place in relation to specific contexts.

With regard to notions of empowerment, the orientations which we utilise also facilitate a move away from the Utopianism or universalism contained in so many of the current discussions. Accordingly, questions are posed as to whether empowerment or empowering strategies can be abstractly and precisely delineated, with universalistic ground rules, outside specific contexts. Similarly, it moves us away from scenarios where empowerment is perceived in an abstract 'them' and 'us' manner and delivered unproblematically from one person to another.

In terms of social work practice in relation to 'carers' and 'caring', we suggest that the implications are for work which seeks clarity rather than certainty, fluidity rather than rigidity and collective negotiations around non-static individual and group identities, rather than static-projected or self-imposed categorisations. We recognise the dangers of sliding into relativism, or focusing on difference and contradiction to such an extent that collective action becomes impossible. This is why we want to maintain reformulated links such as those propounded by Flax, Williams and Fraser and Nicholson. This is not because we want to impose new certainties, but because they provoke thought and point us in useful directions. Flax's emphasis on constraint and unintended consequences, for example, is an important counterbalance to the free-floating Utopianism which accompanied much radical rhetoric around topics such as empowerment. Her emphasis on reviewing and reflecting is a reminder that processes or outcomes are experienced differently by different groups and generations.

We argue for the development of practice initiatives which allow for the discussion of mutuality as well as differences and which are based on norms and rules which are subject to change and negotiation. To draw from Flax:

'In recognising differences as well as mutuality, one is forced to negotiate with others and to see the boundedness of one's claims as well as one's mutual responsibility for and dependence upon the character of the "we" ' (Flax 1992:206/7).

Conclusion

Williams (1992) utilising the work of Boyne and Rattansi (1990) distinguishes between postmodernity as a condition – 'a set of changes, transitions and processes perceived to be taking place at the social, political, economic and cultural levels and postmodernism as a particular shift in theory and analysis which is itself part of the condition' (Williams 1992:204). We argue that post-modern concepts can lead to a focus on undifferentiated pluralism, relativity and superficiality and can have problematic implications. However, we suggest that we do not have to be overwhelmed by the condition and we critique responses which search for certainties and corresponding rigidities, categoricalisations and impositions. We maintain that there are mediating concepts which in varying ways make links between the 'isms' and enable us to weigh competing claims and voices. We also assert that the debates which surround 'caring' and 'carers' can be usefully informed by the acceptance of contradiction, uncertainty and provisionality as dynamic rather than problematic forces.

Notes

[1]Postmodernism and Poststructuralism. The relationship between poststructuralist and postmodern perspectives is far from straightforward and many different writers hold varying viewpoints. Best and Kellner (1991) see critiques of structuralism as forming the theoretical conditions which helped to develop postmodern theory. They regard poststructuralism as part of the matrix of postmodern theory and whilst relating theoretical breaks described as postmodern directly to poststructuralist critiques, interpret poststructuralism 'as a subset of a broader range of theoretical, cultural, and social tendencies which constitute postmodern discourse' (1991:25). Madan Samp (1993) asserts that there are so many similarities between poststructuralist theories and postmodern practices that it is difficult to make a clear distinction between them and Huyssen (1990) inveighs against postmodernism and poststructuralism being seen as relating to a similar broad area. However, for the purposes of this chapter, we draw from Barrett (1992) who maintains that to explore the relationship between contemporary feminist and social theory it is necessary to cite postmodernist as well as poststructuralist arguments.

References

Arber, S. and Gilbert, N. (1993) Men: The Forgotten Carers, in Bornat J.; Pereira C.; Pilgrim D.; and Williams F *Community Care: A Reader* Macmillan/Open University, Basingstoke.

Baistow, K. (1995) Liberation and Regulation? Some Paradoxes of Empowerment in *Critical Social Policy* 1995, Spring: 34 - 46.

Barrett, M. (1987) The Concept of Difference, *Feminist Review* 26, July: 29 - 41

Barrett, M. (1991) *The Politics of Truth: From Marx to Foucault*, Polity Press, Cambridge.

Barrett, M. (1992) Words and Things: Materialism and Method in Contemporary Feminist Analysis in Barrett M. and Phillips A. (Eds.) *Destabilising Theory: Contemporary Feminist Debates*, Polity Press, Cambridge.

Beresford, P. and Croft, S. (1993) *Citizen Involvement: A Practical Guide for Change*, BASW/Macmillan, Basingstoke.

Boyne, R. and Rattansi, D. (1990) *Postmodernism and Society*, London, Macmillan.

Brah, A. (1992) Difference, Diversity and Differentiation in Donald J. and Rattansi A. (Eds.) *'Race', Culture and Difference*, London, Sage.

Braye, S. and Preston-Shoot, M.(1993) Empowerment and Partnership in Mental Health:Towards a Different Relationship in *Journal of Social Work Practice* Vol.7 No.2.1993:115-128.

Croft, S. and Beresford, P. (1990) From Paternalism to Participation: Involving People in *Social Services, Open Services Project*, Joseph Rowntree Foundation.

Dailey, G. (1988) *Ideologies of Caring: Rethinking Community and Collectivism*, Macmillan, London.

Dowson, S. (1990) *Keeping it Safe: Self Advocacy by People with Learning Difficulties and the Professional Response, Values Into Action*, London.

Fawcett, B. and Featherstone, B. (1994) The Implications of Community Care Policies For People Who Require and Use Services, in Care in Place: The *International Journal of Networks and Community*, Routledge 1:2: June 1994: 120-132.

Finch, J. and Grove, D. (1983) (Eds.) *A Labour of Love: Women, Work and Caring*, Routledge and Kegan Paul, London.

Finkelstein, V. (1993) Disability: An Administrative Challenge? (The Health and Welfare Heritage) in Oliver, M. (Eds.) Social Work: Disabled People and Disabling Environments, Research Highlights in *Social Work* 21, Jessica Kingsley, London.

Fisher, M. (1994) Man-made Care: Community Care and Older Male Carers in *British Journal of Social Work*, 24:659-680.

Flax, J. (1990) *Thinking Fragments: Psychoanalysis, Feminism and Postmodernism in the Contemporary West,* University of California Press, Berkeley.

Flax, J. (1992) Beyond Equality: Gender, Justice and Difference in Bock, G. and James, S. *Beyond Equality and Difference* 1992 Routledge, London.

Flax, J. (1993) *Disputed Subjects,* Routledge, London.

Foucault, M. (1979) *Discipline and Punish*, Penguin, Harmondsworth.

Foucault, M. (1981) T*he History of Sexuality Volume One, An Introduction,* Pelican, Harmondsworth.

Foucault, M. (1981) A Question of Method: An Interview with Michel Foucault, *Ideology and Consciousness*, 8: 1-14.

Fraser, N. and Nicholson, L. (1993) Social Criticism Without Philosophy: An Encounter Between Feminism and Postmodernism in Docherty, T. (1993)(Eds) *Postmodernism: A Reader*, Harvester Wheatsheaf, London.

Graham, H. (1993) 'Feminist Perspectives on Caring' in Bornat, J.; Pereira, C.; Pilgrim, D. and Williams, F. (1993) *Community Care: A Reader* Open University/Macmillan, Basingstoke.

Green, H. (1988) *Informal Carers: General Household Survey 1985*, HMSO, London. HMSO , NHS and Community Care Act 1990.

HMSO (1989) White Paper Caring For People: Community Care in the Next Decade and Beyond.

hooks, b. (1991) *Yearning: Race, Gender and Cultural Politics*, Turnaround Press, London.

Howe, D. (1994) Modernity, Postmodernity and Social Work in *British Journal of Social Work* 24: 513 - 532.

Huyssen, A. (1990) Mapping the Postmodern in Nicholson, N. (Ed.) *Feminism, Postmodernism*, Routledge, London.

Lyotard, I .L. (1984) *The Postmodern Condition: A Report on Knowledge* (Trans) Bennington, G. and Massumi, B. University of Minnesota Press, Minneapolis.

Morris, J. (1993) *Pride Against Prejudice*, The Women's Press, London.

Oliver, M. (1990) *The Politics of Disablement*, Macmillan, Basingstoke.

Oliver, M. (1992) *Social Work With Disabled People,* BASW/Macmillan, Basingstoke.

Oliver, M. (1993) (Ed.) *Social Work: Disabled People and Disabling Environments*, Jessica Kingsley, London.

Opie, A. (1992) Qualitative Research, Appropriation of the Other and Empowerment, in *Feminist Review* Nos. 40 - 42: 52 - 69.

PahI, J. (1992) Force for Change an Optional Extra? The Impact of Research on Policy in Social Work and Social Welfare in Carter, P. *et al.* (Eds.) *Changing Social Work and Welfare*, Open University Press, Buckingham.

Parton, N. (1994) Problematics of Government, (Post) Modernity and Social Work in *British Journal Of Social Work* Vol.24 No.1. Feb: 9 - 32.

Qureshi, H. and Walker, A. (1988) *The Caring Relationship*, Routledge and Kegan Paul, London.

Sarup, M. (1993) *Poststructuralism and Postmodernism*, Harvester Wheatsheaf, Hemel Hempstead.

Sawicki, J. (1991) *Disciplining Foucault: Feminism, Power and the Body* Routledge, London.

Solomon, B. (1976) *Black Empowerment: Social Work in Oppressed Communities*, Columbia University Press, New York.

Twigg, J. and Atkin, K. (1994) *Carers Perceived,* Open University Press, Buckingham

Ward, D. and Mullender, A. (1992) Empowerment and Oppression: An Indissoluble Pairing for Contemporary Social Work in *Critical Social Policy* Issue 32, Autumn:21 -30.

Weedon, C. (1987) *Feminist Practice and Poststructuralist Theory*, Blackwell, Oxford.

Williams, F. (1992) Somewhere Over the Rainbow: Universality and Diversity in Social Policy, Manning, N. and Page, R.(1992) (Ed.) *Social Policy Review* 4, Social Policy Association.

Williams, F. (1994) Michele Barrett: *From Marxist to Poststructuralist Feminism in Modern Thinkers on Welfare*, George, V. and Page, R. (Eds.) (1994) Harvester Wheatsheaf, London.

Williams, F. (1995) Postmodernism, Feminism and the Question of Difference, to be published in Parton, N. (Ed.), Routledge 1995/1996

Chapter 5
Yes, But IS IT Empowerment? Initiation, Implementation and Outcomes of Community Action

Jill Anderson

'If you are here to help me then you are wasting your time. But if your liberation is tied up in mine, then let us begin.'[1]

In this chapter I intend to focus on local community groups and suggest questions that should be asked of any community initiative when trying to answer: 'yes, but is it empowerment?' I shall look at initiation, implementation and outcomes of community action, along with the role of professionals, arguing that asking pertinent questions is more important than knowing all the answers. At each stage we need to bear in mind whether a way of acting increases access to knowledge, skills, decisions, networks and resources for those who have least access to these components of power. When considering initiation I will look at who is setting the agenda and defining the problem and within what frameworks of knowledge the problem is seen to lie. I shall then consider implementation, asking who is taking action and what sort of action, including the role of professionals. When considering outcomes I shall ask questions about individual and community gains and losses and what may influence these.

Empowerment: What is it?
All social practices are shaped by power (Foucault in Radtke and Stam 1994) and different perspectives on power shape our understanding of empowerment. The distinction between power-to, as the capacity to act, and power-over, as dominion or domination, is an important starting point (Wallerstein 1992).

Empowerment in its broadest sense can be seen as increasing power-to, especially for marginalised people and groups; those who are farthest down the ladder in the power-over hierarchy and who have least access to knowledge, decisions, networks, and resources (Wang and Burris 1994). As Janeways points out, even the weak are not without power: they have the power to disbelieve; the power to come together as a group to act towards common goals; and they have the power to organise for action. (cited in Radtke and Stam 1994). So resistance to oppressive structures can be seen as an exercise of power, with disempowerment arising from a lack of resistance: 'the succumbing to conditions as they are or appear to be' (Faith 1994 p56).

Wallerstein (1994 p143) points out that 'definitions drive our practice' and she encapsulates many themes when she defines empowerment as 'a social-action process that promotes participation of people, organisations and communities towards the goal of increased individual and community control, political efficacy, improved quality of community life and social justice' (Wallerstein 1992 p198).

This and other definitions include individual and community control. Individual or psychological empowerment can either be seen to be a quality similar to self-esteem, or as feelings of greater control that individuals gain following active membership of organisations. Community empowerment includes this along with political action towards redistribution of resources. (Rissell 1994).

Empowerment as a process, rather than an outcome, is a recurring theme (Bystydzienski 1992, Rappaport 1987, Wallerstein and Bernstein 1994), with many attempts to identify steps in the process so we can tell how far along the route we have travelled. Jacson *et al* and Labonte (both cited in Rissell 1994) identify steps as:

- Personal Development
- Mutual Support Groups
- Issue Identification and Campaigns
- Community Organisation
- Participation in Community Organisations, Coalitions and Advocacy
- Collective Political and Social Action

When asking 'is it empowerment?' we can consider whether we are travelling along this route or not. However, if we see power as exercised in all relations, as Foucault does, rather than as a commodity possessed, 'gaining' power will not be a simple linear progression (cited in Radtke and Stam 1994). The process of empowerment will not mean that all relationships are similarly enhanced. For example, collective political and social action on a particular issue may not enhance the ability to challenge all authorities or increase knowledge of unrelated topics or provide access to all networks.

Despite claims that individual empowerment only occurs with participation in group action, it seems that a certain level of individual power is a necessary first step before any individual can play a part in groups that act in community-empowering ways (Wallerstein 1992). In the West, the most marginalised are not those who spontaneously join with others to act towards a common goal: they are the ones who remain isolated, lacking time, energy, confidence, skills, and money to put into community action; those whose struggle for daily existence wears away the power to resist.

Empowerment is at the heart of health promotion, with claims that powerlessness (subjective and objective) is a risk factor for disease (Eisen 1994, Wallerstein 1992). Increasing individual and community control over life can be seen as a pre-requisite of 'health'. The components that would need to be under control extend from macro-political decisions, for example those related to resource distribution, rights, and equality, to the environment we live in (pollution, crime, housing), to resources available to us (money, time, energy), to the information available to us. Linking empowerment to health raises questions over whether empowerment is an assumed good or whether we have to show positive impacts on physical and mental health, and reductions in demand on health and caring systems, to justify empower-ing processes and actions.

Initiation: Who defines the problem?
Who decides there is a need for community action, in response to which perceived problems? A simplified dichotomy of 'professionals / outsiders' and 'community members' may overlook ways of defining problems that can empower and those that do not. For community initiatives to contribute towards empowerment there is a need for community ownership of definitions of problems and of strategies for solutions. Kenner (1986) claims that self-definition of need makes every initiative unique.

Those defining needs can be responding to their own needs: to 'help', to gain recognition; or to their interpretation of others' needs, what they think those needs are or ought to be. As Eisen points out to practitioners: 'never assume you know the needs and priorities of people; confess your utter ignorance of their back-ground and the way their minds work, the reasons for their attitudes and ask them how they would like you to help' (Eisen 1994 p250).

An important consideration is: to what extent is the local community involved in defining the problem and constructing solutions? Wilcox (1994 p78) argues that one of the greatest barriers to local action is 'not invented here'. Wilcox discusses different levels of participation in decision-making, representing varying degrees of citizen power. The lowest level of participation is that of information: members of the community and of groups are simply told what is planned. Consultation of communities is frequently at the level of offering options, listening to feedback but not allowing new ideas. When community groups and community members are involved with professionals in deciding and acting together a greater degree of ownership will be present. When professionals support independent community interests without imposing an outside agenda this encourages a greater level of citizen power. So when asking is it empowerment? we could consider the level of citizen power and involvement in agenda setting.

The question of 'who is the community?' will be vital when considering whose needs and demands are taken into account when problems are identified and acted upon and there can be conflicting agendas. Guttierez contrasts community efforts to incorporate and support disabled people in a neighbourhood with community efforts to block the construction of a group home for disabled people (Guttierez 1994).

Whether women and/or men are involved in decision making can make a difference to how needs are defined and acted upon. Different groups within a community may choose to act separately on their own self-defined needs (e.g. Black people, women, elders). As Kenner (1986) points out, this self-chosen separatism must be distinguished from an imposed segregation from the mainstream.

Defining the problem may put it in the realm of the individual or firmly base it in the socio-political context. The dilemma is that if we focus on changing individuals to better cope with a sick society we neglect analysis of root causes and may even diffuse the impetus for social change, but individuals who are 'coping' better with their lives have more energy to put into groups and campaigns that push for change. For example, an individual approach that failed to address root causes occurred in a programme with women living in poverty in the USA offering training in budgeting skills, job searching, stress management and nutrition (Thurston 1989). It failed to consider how 'budgeting' an inadequate amount of money, searching for non-existent jobs, and knowing about nutrition while being unable to buy adequate food, could simply add to the stress the women were being trained to manage. This tendency to individualise and pathologise just responses to unjust situations sees the problem lying with feckless and inadequate individuals who are in poverty because of their own deficiencies, rather than questioning the structures that inevitably lead to haves and have-nots.

Professionals may have a role to play in putting the problem into a wider context. For example, in South Africa a nurse responded to the high incidence of wife battering by encouraging the women to come together to discuss their situations and the reasons for male violence (Nelson 1992). She was in a position to have more information about the extent of the problem from her frequent dealings with 'victims', whereas individual women had remained isolated through fear and shame. Coming together is an important first step that does not necessarily lead to action and concrete changes.

However, the fact that professionals have different knowledge to the communities they work with and the idea that this knowledge is superior, creates a power difference. Whereas sharing information would seem to address this, we must be aware of how knowledge is generated, within which frameworks it is analysed and who owns knowledge, a valuable commodity. Ownership of knowledge is ascribed to the 'academy' (Malterud 1993) and this ownership is enforced by being communicated in language impenetrable to the uninitiated and by being kept in academic institutions, such as university libraries that non-members do not have access to.

Professionals can occasionally act to subvert the ownership of knowledge by passing privileged information to the people they work with, though of course this could be risky. For instance, in a recent research project carried out to elicit local perceptions of education needs, the researchers had a confidentiality clause in their contract forbidding sharing any information that they obtained. However, the researchers designed the research to include sending copies of the first draft report to over one hundred participants in the research, so bypassing the restriction on information (Anderson and Hutton 1994).

The theoretical frameworks for analysis of social and political reality are based on untestable assumptions (Rappaport 1987) and require an act of faith that shapes perceptions, the interpretation of observations and data, and the search for meaning (Kuhn cited in Rappaport 1987). As Connells points out, power includes the control of definitions and the understanding of situations (cited in Radtke and Stam 1994). So 'whose knowledge?' and 'whose power?' are important considerations. NEZDHI (1991) in the former Soviet Union argue that one of the foundations of patriarchy is men's monopoly of information and knowledge. When communities participate in knowledge production in their own terms this can of itself be empowering (Freire cited in Chesler 1991) but must address the way knowledge is appropriated and analysed in closeted circles.

The form this participation takes is important. Those actively participating in gathering information from and about their local community will gain skills, confidence and knowledge of the research process. This can go some way towards demystifying research and what counts for knowledge. But if the information so gained is simply whisked away to be written up in academic language and become the property of outsiders, then control lies elsewhere.

If one of the powers of the weak is the power to disbelieve, then a healthy scepticism would seem to be vital for communities having their problems defined for them, as well as for professionals working with them. As Pivens and Cloward point out the power of beliefs 'defines for people . . . what is possible and what is impossible' (quoted in Haussman 1992 page 110). In Nepal, Freirean literacy classes with local women began by identifying key words in the lives of the women through discussion. This led to the women naming one of their key problems as male violence in the home and in public spaces. This 'knowledge' was generated by the women themselves and acted as a spur for action to publicly humiliate the perpetrators and to offer support and protection to the women affected (Parajuli and Enslin 1990). The scope of solutions, of what was possible, changed as the women increased their confidence, their strength and the power of their voices.

Initiation: Is empowerment just rhetoric?

Community empowerment can be a very powerful and therefore a very dangerous political strategy. Those with power-over will inevitably try to depoliticise by appropriation of the terms and definitions. Open opposition to community action may fuel protest and campaigns, whereas tokenism in taking on empowerment can diffuse activism by individualising it, or by using empowerment strategies in top-down, disempowering ways. For example, empowerment can be seen as 'the professionals response to community demands for increased control over their own health' (Rissell 1994).

It is important to look at who is using the term and ask what their aims are in doing so. If the term is used to justify policies that primarily aim to save money, cut back on services and shift blame, then this embodies an attempt to depoliticise the word. When community effort is put into maintaining provisions where services are withdrawn (e.g. care in the community?) this can eat up time and energy for community action. The despair generated by stepwise backward movement in social justice, for example in Britain and the USA, can lead to incremental erosion of resistance and apathy.

Responsibility, as in 'we are each responsible for our own health', without control of the determinants of health, victimises by victim-blaming. It is control, rather than responsibility, that is inherent in empowerment. When claims are made that 'care in the community' is empowering, we need to ask who is being asked to provide what services for free that were previously provided by the State. Is this merely burdening those with least access to resources with the care of elderly, sick and disabled relatives? However, as Morris points out, the division of 'carer' and 'cared for' blurs the relationship of caring (Morris 1993). Who is empowerment for? The cared for or the carer? So is it empowerment to be released from insti-tutional care into a hostile community with no family to provide alternatives? Is it empowerment to be on call 24 hours a day to tend the needs of an ill or disabled relative? Is it empowerment when budget restrictions limit what can be provided to case the plight of the (un)cared for?

Implementation: Who is taking action?

Most agree that empowerment occurs in action of some kind. Who is taking action and what action is being taken are important considerations. The generalisation of 'the local community' taking action obscures the reality of who is acting, whose time and energy are being used to benefit which sections of the community, and at what cost. Wallerstein (1992) points out that to become involved in the change process, a minimum perceived individual power was necessary, so the most powerless are not the key participants. Moser, however, argues that women, as an extension of their domestic role, often take on responsibility for 'formation, orga-nization and success of local level protest groups' (Moser 1989 p200). She also points out that women's involvement is frequently at the level of community managing for collective consumption and is usually unpaid. Men's involvement tends to be in community leadership roles, informal political organizations and is more likely to be paid. It is important to note that 'voluntary' is often a euphemism for unpaid. Women's time, energy, enthusiasm and commitment to collective action are frequently given for free in spite of (or perhaps because of) their many other commitments. Perhaps it is assumed that women gain individual empower-ment as an adequate reward making it unnecessary to pay them in other ways.

In a project in China, women were given cameras and training in photography to record their everyday lives. These portrayals acted as stimulators of discussion of their reality, and as a means to feed into policy their self-defined problems. This project provided the women with a subsidy equal to the amount of field wages they would lose in order to participate fully 'we never assumed that the village women had extra time on their hands, nor that their everyday work responsibilities were easy' (Wang and Burris 1994 p184).

Implementation: What is the role of the professional?

Q.   How many community development workers does it take to change a
      lightbulb?

A.   None – the community becomes empowered to change its own light bulbs.

So what is the role of the professional working with communities? Labonte asks whether it is possible to empower anyone else (Labonte 1994).

Gruber and Tricket point out that 'there is a fundamental paradox in the idea of people empowering others because the very institutional structures that put one group in a position to empower also work to undermine the act of empowerment' (quoted in Rissell 1994 p240). However, there are certain ways in which professionals can aid the process, rather than hampering it: by helping with practicalities and acting as a resource; by facilitating empowerment education; by acting as a channel to policy; and by becoming an ally.

1. Practicalities
Meeting practical needs to support community action may include help with funding, space to meet, access to photocopying, or access to information and knowledge (e.g. about rights or power channels). However, if funding or resources come with strings it may act to limit the scope and effectiveness of any action.

Many practitioners act on the practicalities of the lives of their individual clients, 'helping' with, e.g. liaising with, bureaucracies on their behalf, counselling, arranging child-care or training. This may enable the most burdened to participate more fully with other people or may simply create further dependency. The way this help is given and how clients have participated in defining their own needs are both important in this respect.

2. Facilitating empowerment education
Empowerment education is based on Freire's approach to education for liberation from oppression. This approach uses themes and ideas of importance to the group of learners. These themes are presented to the group in the form of codes (e.g. pictures, stories, drama, songs) that aim to pose a problem rather than provide answers. The codes act both to stimulate discussion about familiar situations and their root causes, and to generate responses and solutions that people can communally employ to improve their lives. Action and reflection on that action together enhance critical thinking and affect the way people perceive their lives; moving from helpless recipients of oppressive structures to active agents rewriting the world (Barnett 1992).

Empowerment education can be seen as a process of 'learning to perceive social, political and economic contradictions and to take action against the oppressive elements of reality'. (Freire quoted in Mies 1983). This process may or may not be facilitated by professionals. When practitioners engage in this process as partners, learning about their own prejudices, racism and institutions (Rissell 1994) then there is some scope for success. For professionals to effectively facilitating empowerment education it is necessary for them to subvert the bureaucratic structures of which they are a part.

As Wallerstein (1992) points out, there are a number of assumptions about empowerment education and she asks us to question these:

> The first is that participation leads to changed perceptions. The nature and level of participation, from manipulation to ownership, will determine whether 'participation' will positively affect the way people view their lives and possibilities.

> The second assumption is that mobilising in community groups will strengthen networks. The nature of the group will be an important determinant: Is it democratic? How are power, decision making and workload distributed within the group? Are they always the same voices and the same people doing all the work? Groups can quickly become cliques that do not encourage new membership, that only strengthen networks for a few chosen members.

> The third assumption is that empowerment education promotes improvements in environment or health conditions. If this is to be so then that education must increase control over resources, environment, knowledge and decisions.

In theory, the process of empowerment includes a push for social change, once critical consciousness allows perception of injustice and of ways to counteract it. But might facilitators of empowerment education have their own agenda, their own ideas of what is just and unjust, that become, even subtly, imposed upon communities? It seems that androcentric, white, middle-class, liberal expectations and ways of behaving intrude, so communities are seen to be acting in empowering ways when they strive for a white middle-class version of the good life-gaining more local resources within existing power structures. Brock-Utna argues that this is not enough: 'we do not want a piece of the pie, we want to change the recipe of the pie' (quoted in Bystydzienski 1992 page 14).

As Parajuli and Enslin (1990 p54) point out, 'Empowerment education should reveal the conflicting interpretation of knowledge between dominant and subordinate groups'. Conflicting goals of different subordinate groups should also become apparent.

Empowerment is often central to health promotion. When a community development approach is used to tap into local needs and respond to them by assisting group formation, recognising local skills and facilitating empowerment education, then it is possible that it is empowerment. However, more frequently a preset health agenda exists which does not allow people to define their own priorities.

Government strategies such as 'Health of the Nation' (which have a strong influence on where funding goes) define problems nationally and so restrict local definitions of what is important, while conspicuously omitting poverty as a health issue (Department of Health 1992).

In a project in the USA learners participated in developing their own learning materials to act as codes but the health agenda had already been set, for example teenage smoking or cleaning up the local environment. There were attempts to address other issues of concern to participants, such as racism or unemployment, but the primary aim of the material was to raise issues considered by professionals to be of key importance (Rudd and Coming 1994).

An example of empowerment education leading to effective action comes from Andhra Pradesh, India. A literacy class with rural women began by identifying issues of importance to the women. The local cheap alcohol was seen to be a source of many problems, contributing to economic hardship, drunkenness and violence inside and outside the home. The women discussed the problem and ways of tackling it. They took direct action by putting nails on roads to stop deliveries and damaged shops that sold alcohol. This rural campaign spread to other women including the urban élite and addressed issues including men's role in the family. This action resulted in a state-wide ban on alcohol (Thakur 1995).

3. A channel to policy

Practitioners can act as a channel, translating community feelings and demands into policies. However, when practitioners see their role solely in terms of writing policy plans without having regular contact with community groups and members, they can easily become divorced from reality and act in top-down ways: defining community problems and needs instead of listening and responding.

This raises issues of accountability and efficiency. Professionals in hierarchies are usually only accountable 'upwards' to their line managers and rarely to their clients. Dissatisfied clients and groups may have to jump through fire to complain or have their dissatisfaction acted upon. A concern with efficiency in the current climate means professionals and others are 'less likely to patiently elicit leadership from others' (Silverman 1994): it is always quicker, easier, 'more efficient' to do it for them than to enable them to do it for themselves.

4. An ally

Perhaps the most important role of professionals is as an ally, both in the sense of uniting in common interests and in the sense of offering support. This would include advocating in policy channels (as above) and facilitating new channels by making links with other groups around wider issues. The support offered to new and existing groups would include practicalities listed above along with emotional and affirming support.

It is possible that those who choose freely to communally live outside of society's norms have the best chances: for example, travellers, squatter camps such as Greenham Common, religious communities such as Findhorn in Scotland, who attempt to establish structures that are empowering to their membership while exploring alternatives. Professionals who attempt to educate for reintegration into the mainstream (the get-a-job, pay-your-bills, money-is-all society) may be hindering empowerment by assuming all children should go to school to compete and that all sickness needs medical attention. When professionals are expected to police the system they are not in a position to support those choosing to live outside of it. Professionals can further punish those with alternative lifestyles by taking children away from their parents 'for their own good', by treating them as sick, mad or criminal, by denying they have a right to make their own decisions. Taking the side of those you work with may be considered subversion by hierarchies in which professionals work. Supporting freely chosen decisions not to become 'respectable' members of society may also require a huge leap of faith.

Implementation: What sort of action?
There is a need for a variety of solutions, a multiplicity of tactics and strategies in different settings. Wallerstein (1992) claims that there is no perfect model, no rules about how to 'do' empowerment. Rappaport (1987) claims that locally developed solutions are inherently more empowering. There is a need for inventiveness and creativity to constantly discover new approaches.

The techniques employed by groups to address their own defined needs will necessarily be richly varied. When the need is seen for increasing access to the political process for less powerful groups such as women, a huge diversity of approaches has been used in different localities, cultures and countries. Bystydzienski summarises some of these as: involvement in makeshift organisations and self-help groups; organising protests; developing informal networks and coalitions; drawing on existing groups (Bystydzienski (1992). Najar (1992) lists strategies employed by Palestinian women's committees attempting to ensure that the liberation struggle includes an improvement in the position of women. These include mass recruitment, participation in local committees, education and literacy, financial empowerment through vocational training, employment and co-operatives, provision of child-care and health services, encouraging solidarity with other groups such as the families of martyrs, making contact with international and Israeli women's groups, using women's publications to promote discussion and acknowledge women's contribution, and participating in the national struggle.

What are the outcomes?

With empowerment as process, what is the outcome? Empowering social action at a local level will not always lead to noticeable positive social change. Labonte (1994) argues that when we view the community as locality, we may ignore national and transnational impacts that occur via economic and social policy. Wallerstein (1992) argues that fluid social situations mean that empowered communities may at some times influence the larger picture and not at others, seeing empowerment as the ability to judge situations and decide whether current conditions seem appropriate to demand change. However, an unfavourable macro-political climate may mean that different strategies are called for. For example, if a fairer resource distribution through taxation and social spending seems unlikely, local communities can develop resource and skill-sharing schemes such as food co-operatives and Local Exchange Trading Schemes (LETS). Again, absence of resistance, of action against oppression, can be seen as most disempowering. Although only small effects may be seen from local initiatives, Eisen (1994) argues that a critical mass of activity from numerous small initiatives will lead to restoration of the social fabric. Perhaps this is a bit optimistic. A recent survey by Black of one hundred local initiatives in Britain found the most successful schemes acted by tackling day-to-day practicalities while also acting at a strategic level with a firm political agenda. While acknowledging that long-term gains are difficult to gauge, Black found that many of the 100 groups were in a rut, with volunteers and workers 'giving up' when faced with recurrent crises especially over funding (Black cited in Moore 1995).

Empowerment action towards one goal may or may not have influence on other areas of life. There may be some progress along the process but no concrete or visible outcome. The same group may sometimes seem able to push for change and not at other times.

When looking at outcomes, we have to ask who gains and who loses. Although empowerment is seen as a wholly positive process, it is possible that some groups can become empowered at the expense of others (Wallerstein and Bernstein 1994) especially when there are multiple, conflicting needs within a community. So if we look to the local community to define their own successes we must be mindful to include the views of the housebound, those not participating in groups, those on the fringes, and not simply the views of those active in groups.

In the case of Andhra Pradesh mentioned earlier women organised to prohibit the sale of cheap alcohol and achieved this goal. Whether this has resulted in the alcohol industry going underground is unclear. Whether or not the previous consumers of alcohol (mainly men) feel this is a positive is not recorded (Thakur 1995).

Social change may benefit many people in a community, particularly those who participated in social action. Those individuals who give time and energy may gain most, in terms of increased skills, confidence and sense of individual power, however, the challenge is to maintain a commitment over time despite set-backs and frustrations that can increase the sense of powerlessness rather than decrease it (Wallerstein and Bernstein 1994).

When empowered communities push for fairer distribution of finite resources within society, achieving this would inevitably mean someone somewhere losing out, even if those with very much would not miss a bob or two they still have a vested interest in maintaining the *status quo*.

Because of this, there is a need for justifiable paranoia in recording positive community initiatives. While positive case studies can give heart to embattled communities and point the way forward, those with power-over are unlikely to sit back and let radical change happen unchallenged. Examples in the literature can indicate ways to preclude social action as well as ways to encourage it. It is possible that projects that are effective are necessarily unrecorded and remain effective only because they are not made public and have eluded close scrutiny. LETS schemes in Britain. which rely for their success on being outside the tax system. have recently come under scrutiny by the Inland Revenue with suggestions that a nominal monetary value is given to the trading units for tax purposes, thus extending the scope of power-over to maintain the *status quo*.

If we are looking at success in terms of policy changes at the national level in response to community demands, it is worth bearing in mind Wildivski's dictum: 'each policy solution is the beginning of the next problem, and success is when the next problem is smaller than the problem for which it is the solution' (quoted in Labonte 1994 p266).

If community action is improving life by providing new services or resources, then it can be seen as a positive outcome. Too often. however, action is mitigating negative social changes. 'Volunteers' providing services withdrawn by the State is not obviously positive. Fighting repeatedly to stop services being withdrawn. such as campaigns against hospital closures, is not a move forward. Campaigns to stop rights being eroded, such as against the Criminal Justice Act, rarely increase rights. Action to prevent environmental disasters, such as against nuclear power or motorways, only has to fail once. Although these demonstrate the power to resist, and people acting communally on self-defined problems, even when successful they seldom result in a positive redistribution of resources or power. When asking 'yes. but is it empowerment?' the answers are seldom simple or unequivocal.

Notes
[1] Anonymous Aborigine woman quoted in Labonte 1994 p258

References
Anderson, J. and Hutton, F. (1994) *All Age Learning Needs in Hulme* Unpublished research report.

Barnett, L. (1992) Pictures as discussion starters *Learning for Health* 1, 8-11.

Bystydzienski, J. M. (1992) Influence of women's culture on public politics in Norway in Bystydzienski J.M. (ed) *op. cit.*.

Bystydzienski, J. M. (ed) (1992) *Women Transforming Politics: Worldwide Strategies for Empowerment* Indiana University Press. Bloomington and Indianapolis.

Chesler, M A. (1991) Participatory Action Research with self-help groups: an alter-native paradigm for enquiry and action *American Journal of Community Psychology* 19/5 759-768.

Department of Health (1992) *Health of the Nation - A Summary Strategy for Health in England* HMSO.

Eisen, A. (1994) Survey of neighbourhood based, comprehensive community empowerment: reflections on professional practice *Health Education Quarterly* 21/2 235-252.

Faith, K. (1994) Resistance: lessons from Foucault and feminism in Radtke. H. L. and Stam, H. J.(eds) Power/Gender: Social Relations in *Theories and Practice*. Sagen Publications. London.

Guttierez, L. (1994) Empowerment forum *Health Education Quarterly* 21/3 283.

Haussman, M. H. (1992) The personal is constitutional in Bystydzienski J. M. *op.cit.*

Kenner, C. (1986) *Whose Needs Count? Community Action for Health* Bedford Square Press.

Labonte, R. (1994) Health promotion and empowerment: reflections on professional practice *Health Education Quarterly* 21/2 253-268.

Malterud, K. (1993) Strategies for empowering women's voices in the medical culture *Health Care for Women International* 14 365-373

Mies, M. (1983) Towards a methodology for feminist research in Bowles, G. and Klein, R. D.(eds) *Theories of Women 's Studies.*

Moore, W. (1995) A hundred ways to healthy living *Guardian* 26/4/95

Morris, J (1993) 'Us' and 'Them'? Feminist research and community care in Bomat *et al: op. cit.*

Najjar, 0. A. (1992) Between nationalism and feminism: the Palestinian answer in Bystydzienski, J. M. *op. cit.*

Nelson, S. (1992) Combining research and action: The Alexandra Action Group Against Women Abuse *GADU Newspack* (Oxfam) No 15.

Parajuli, P. and Enslin, E. (1990) From learning literacy to regenerating women's space: a story of women's empowerment from *Nepal Convergence* xxiii/1 44-55.

Radtke, H. L. and Stam H. J.(eds) (1994) *Power/Gender: Social Relations in Theories and Practice* Sage Publications. London.

Rappaport, J. (1987) Terms of empowerment/exemplars of prevention: towards a theory for community psychology *American Journal of Community Psychology* 15/2 121-148.

Rissell, C. (1994) Empowerment: the holy grail of health promotion? *Health Promotion International* 9/1: 39-47.

Rudd, R. E. and Coming, J. P. (1994) Learner developed materials: an empowering product *Health Education Quarterly* 21/3 313-327.

Silverman, E. L. (1994) Women in women''s organizations: power or pouvoir in Radtke, H. L. and Stam, H. J. *op. cit.*

Thakur, S. (1995) Women's Hour. BBC Radio 4 10/4/95.

Thurston, L. P.(1989) Women surviving: an alternative approach to 'helping' low income urban women *Women and Therapy* 8/4 109-127.

Wallerstein, N. (1992) Powerlessness, empowerment and health: implications for health promotion programs *American Journal of Health Promotion* 6/3 197-205.

Wallerstein, N. and Bernstein, E. (1994) Introduction to community empowerment, participatory education and health *Health Education Quarterly* 21/2 141 - 149.

Wang, C. and Burris, M.A. (1994) Empowerment through photo novella: portraits of participation *Health Education Quarterly* 21/2 171-186.

Wilcox, D. (1994) Community participation and empowerment: putting theory into practice *RRA notes* 21 78-82 Institute for Environment and Development: Sustainable Agriculture Programme.

Chapter 6
Empowerment and the Politics of Poverty

Tony Novak

As the twentieth century draws to a close poverty has re-emerged as perhaps the greatest economic, social and political challenge that we face. It is a problem that affects not only millions of people in the so-called Third World but also millions more in the rich countries of the industrialised west. It is, moreover, a problem of growing rather than diminishing proportions. Even as individual countries get richer, more people are becoming poorer: in many parts of the world, Britain included, the poor are worse off than they were ten or twenty years ago. As divisions between rich and poor both between and within individual countries – harden, and as unfettered market forces come to dominate the world economy, the marginalisation and exclusion of the poor from the benefits of economic progress and growth look set to create ever greater misery, tension and strife.

Poverty is a problem the effects of which are felt in a myriad of different ways: in hunger and early death, in poor health, despair and depression, in the corrosion of people's well-being and social relationships, and in frustration and anger. As such, poverty lies at the root of and contributes significantly to many other social problems, to growing levels of social tension, to racism and other forms of violence. It is a problem of immense proportions, both in the numbers whose lives are disfigured by it and in the scale and nature of change required to eradicate it. Yet the eradication of poverty is perfectly possible. For the first time in human history the world has enough resources to meet the basic requirements of human need across the globe. In this sense, poverty is not an economic problem: it is not the result of economic scarcity. On the contrary, global capitalism in the late twentieth century has the means – if not the will – to abolish poverty, and the potential – if resources were directed to that end rather than squandered on unproductive expenditure on armaments, or in the enforced unemployment of 140 million and underemployment of nearly 1,000 million people worldwide – to provide a comfortable life for all. The problem then is not an economic, but a political one. It is about power and control over resources, and the solution to the problem – fundamental and long-term though it may be – can only be to return that power to those who have been dispossessed of it.

Who are the poor?

How we think, and how we are encouraged to think, about poverty has enormous implications for this project. The massive injustice and inequalities of poverty, its destruction of human well-being and spirit, have been and remain the greatest indictment of social and economic progress and the so-called civilisation of contemporary societies. The protection of the interests of those who benefit from this situation has created a set of ideologies and practices through which this reality – and its potential for a revolutionary challenge to the existing structures of wealth and power – is constantly denied. For over a 100 years the tendency in the West has been to see the poor as an isolated, small and largely culpable minority. The isolation of the poor reflects a number of political processes that we shall consider later, but it also includes a way of looking at the poor that sees them as separate from the rest of the society around them and of poverty as capable of being understood without reference to this wider context. The portrayal of the poor as a small (sometimes growing, sometimes shrinking) minority similarly reflects a tendency to view poverty primarily in terms of income, and to measure it by means of an often meagre poverty line. The culpability of the poor – the view that they are largely to blame for their own situation – again builds upon the development over many generations of theories, explanations and ideologies which reflect the interests of those with power rather than the reality of the poor themselves

Poverty cannot be understood in isolation, although many studies of poverty take this approach, looking at the poor as a discrete object of inquiry without reference to their relationships with the wider society. Poverty is always in a relationship with wealth: to see it otherwise is like having a concept of short without having a concept of tall. It is moreover a relationship between social groups: between those who have wealth and power over resources and those who do not.

Viewed in this context, who counts as poor is a highly controversial and political issue. It has been customary throughout the twentieth century to measure – and indeed to define – poverty by reference to a more or less agreed (but frequently contested) poverty line based on an assumed minimum level of income necessary in any particular society for physical survival. Such measurements, which for political reasons tend towards the lowest possible figure on which agreement can be reached, themselves encourage a sharp distinction between those who are considered to be poor and those, even just above this line, who are not. Apart from the problem of who is to decide what is a 'necessary' minimum standard of living – and this is something on which the poor themselves are rarely consulted – such attempts to define and measure poverty by reference to a minimum level of income seriously underestimate the extent and experience of poverty (Novak 1995).

Poverty cannot be understood, and is not experienced, in terms of income alone. Poverty is a relationship: it is a relationship ultimately to wealth, but is mediated through people's experiences of the labour market, of state bureaucracies, of the family and patriarchy, or racism. It involves complex patterns of power and powerlessness, multiple facets of deprivation, and issues of humiliation and self-respect. Such experiences cannot be measured, cannot be understood, solely in terms of income. Indeed, a growing number of studies of poverty in the third world have pointed to the centrality of factors other than income in the way that the poor themselves define the problem of poverty. According to one account:

> Of twenty-two poor informants with whom Tony Beck held long discussions in a village in West Bengal, nineteen 'did not hesitate in saying that for them respect was more important than food, and that "without respect food won't go into the stomach".' And Beck added, 'If this feeling is widespread among the poor in India, then planners' and academics' exclusive interest in income and nutrition is inadequate for understanding poverty' (Chambers 1994 p10).

Poverty is a relationship in which a significant part of the population faces conditions of powerlessness, of insecurity and uncertainty: a constant struggle to make ends meet, an unending pressure that substitutes survival for living. A poverty line may well measure who are the poorest, but the conditions of poverty are far more widespread, and the numbers of people who feel or fear its icy draught – whose lives would be improved by its eradication – form a formidable majority in any country.

Yet poverty is something from which people constantly seek to escape, and from which many make strenuous efforts to distance themselves. This is hardly surprising. It is not just the material conditions of poverty which make it unbearable, but the social stigma attached to it that can lead even the poorest to define themselves as not poor. This stigma is in part the product of years of ideology that have laid the blame for poverty on the poor themselves. In a society where, contrary to the evidence, the prevailing message is that hard work will lead to material success, those who don't succeed are branded as lazy, work-shy, incapable and incompetent. Such a message is not the product of ideology alone, but is powerfully reinforced by the ways in which the poor are treated. From even before the Industrial Revolution the State's response to poverty has been to treat the poor as pariahs, as scroungers and as immoral and amoral outcasts deserving only of the most grudging and minimal support (Novak 1988).

The reaction of the poor against such treatment and their refusal to submit to the punishments of the workhouse or the means test have over the past hundred years forced the State in part to give way. Yet important though those victories have been, it is equally important to recognise the ways in which the State, in giving way to some, has created new divisions and reinforced distinctions between the so-called 'deserving' and 'undeserving' poor. In this sense the poor are not treated as an homogeneous bloc, but have been increasingly fragmented and divided – old against young, married against unmarried, white against black, working against non-working poor – and set in competition against one another. This fragmentation of both the experience of, and the potential opposition to, poverty, with its false hierarchies of need and desert, is an issue of fundamental importance for the empowerment of the poor.

The experience of poverty

The stigma of poverty is impossible to escape. No matter how much people may resist it, how wrong they may feel its message to be, it is always there. It is particularly present in people's dealings with the State. In general the poor are treated poorly, and often with contempt. Poor neighbourhoods are not just neighbourhoods of poor people, but poorly designed, poorly built and poorly serviced. Poor people work in poor environments at poor jobs that offer little variety, few opportunities for expression, and increased risks to physical and mental well-being (Townsend 1979). Those who cannot work necessarily depend upon a benefit system that frequently treats them with suspicion and distrust, requires them to disclose intimate and personal details to strangers behind wired screens, and places them in a position of utter dependency on a bureaucracy that frequently gets things wrong. The poorest are constantly under surveillance, whether from the police, welfare professionals, housing officials, social security investigators or other agents of the State. In schools, hospitals, clinics, recreational and other public facilities, the message is overwhelmingly the same: poor people don't count, and resisting this message is a constant battle for self-respect.

Poverty is time-consuming, yet the poor are often treated as if time were of no consequence. Walking or waiting for a bus to travel to an appointment, to be told to join another queue, or sent to another office to queue and wait again is a common experience. It is this that adds to the experience of the poor that they are invisible: that their urgencies and needs, their very existence as human beings, are nothing compared with the decisions, priorities and whims of those who hold power over them.

Even where the poor are not treated with such obvious contempt they are frequently faced with a condescension that is not far removed from it. It is as if the poor are seen as incapable of understanding their own situation, or themselves of knowing what needs to be done about it. Poor people are not stupid, although they are frequently treated as if they are. It is the ignorance of many of those who seek to 'help' the poor that is the problem, and it is the lack of respect for the poor which dominates the powerlessness of poverty.

This lack of respect is reflected in – and to a considerable degree influenced by – dominant models and explanations of poverty. In general these models portray the poor as deficit individuals or communities. Whether poverty is seen as the result of individual failings – a lack of intelligence, of motivation and drive – or as the result of cultural pathology – a set of behaviour and attitudes passed on from generation to generation – the poor are seen as lacking something.

Models of the poor as deficient underpin many policy interventions. In their more benign forms they point to a need for more education and for a variety of other measures to make up the deficiency. Health education is a classic example. In the face of overwhelming evidence that the poorer people are, the worse their health is likely to be, government ministers and welfare agencies have responded with the exhortation that the poor need to learn to eat better food and live healthier lifestyles. It is their ignorance rather than their poverty which is seen as the problem. Yet research shows clearly that the poor are well aware of what constitutes a healthy diet. The problem is not that of a lack of knowledge, but the lack of the means to do anything about it (Dobson *et al.* 1994).

This approach reaches its most sinister and dangerous heights in recent attempts to portray the poor – or at least significant sections of the poor – as a growing and threatening 'underclass'. Here the poor are seen not only as deficient in the 'normal' values that society as a whole is held to subscribe to – values of family life, of respect for the law and authority, or belief in the work ethic – but are held to have developed 'abnormal' values and patterns of behaviour that actively oppose them. As a concept of social analysis, the notion of an 'underclass' has been criticised (Dean 1991; Vincent 1993; Morris 1994), both for its lack of empirical evidence and for its theoretical weakness, but as part of a growing ideology of poverty it is coming to be established firmly on the policy agenda. Viewed in such a light, the so-called 'underclass' are seen as an active threat – a 'disease' – that threatens to contaminate others, that will not disappear with the growing prosperity of the rest of society, and that therefore calls for punitive measures designed at best to contain their growth, and at worst to confine and eventually to eradicate them as individuals from society altogether.

What is to be done?
One of the first questions that needs to be asked by those who would seek to resolve the problem of poverty is 'who is the problem?' It is now becoming increasingly accepted that in understanding other forms of discrimination and oppression such as racism or sexism or the treatment of disabled people, the focus has to be not on the characteristics of black people, of women or of the disabled themselves, but on the racism of white society, the attitudes of men and the impact of male structures of power, and the ways that society constructs the problems of disability. When dealing with poverty the focus equally needs to move away from looking at poor people as 'the problem' and instead to examine the ways in which structures of power create the problem and experience of poverty. As one writer on Third World poverty has written:

> The objects of development are anyway the poor, not us. It is they who are the problem, not us. We are the solution. So we hold the spotlight to them (from a safe distance). The poor have no spotlight to hold to us. But poverty and deprivation are functions of polarisation, of power and powerlessness. Any practical analysis has to examine the whole system: 'us', the powerful, as well as 'them' the powerless. Since we have more power to act, it is hard to evade the imperative to turn the spotlight round and look at ourselves (Chambers 1994 p7).

One of the important questions here is how far action to alleviate poverty reinforces rather than challenges these structures and relationships of power. Too often, and for all their good intentions, organisations and individuals campaigning against poverty seek to represent the poor, and in representing the poor tend to perpetuate the passivity and powerlessness of the poor themselves.

This has been most evidently true in relation to poverty in the Third World, where charities and other organisations have used images of the poor as helpless passive victims in order to appeal for assistance. Such images reinforce many stereotypes about the poor. They also add to the dominant belief about where the problem lies. The changes in recent years amongst a number of these organisations who have pointed instead to the developed world's exploitation of the poorest countries and to the immense burden of Third World debt have therefore been important, challenging as they do not only images of the poor but also dominant explanations for the causes of world poverty.

In Britain the activities of many campaigning groups have similarly sought to speak on behalf of the poor and to represent their interests to those with power. Important work has been done in lobbying to defend their interests, in securing amendments to legislation and in keeping issues of poverty in the public domain. But such activities have ultimately proved limited in a harsher political climate and have failed to prevent the remorseless spread of poverty. Moreover, to the extent that they attempt to speak for the poor – and in particular as they represent the poor as passive victims seeking people's compassion – they risk confirming stereotypes and reproducing the existing relationships of power. As Peter Beresford and Suzy Croft have argued:

> Its appeal to altruism and benevolence invites approval. But unintentionally or otherwise, this approach emphasises and exaggerates the difference and distance between poor and non-poor people. It rests on an assumption that we should do something for or about them. This implicit 'them' and 'us' of anti-poverty action is divisive and may inadvertently be reinforcing its more clearly negative counterpart on the Right, where 'we' are being drained, damaged and attacked by 'them'. (Beresford & Croft 1995 p3)

In activities such as social work or other professional interventions in poverty, the temptation to represent the poor is even greater. Welfare agencies tend to respond much more readily – in applications for a Social Fund loan, for assistance from the housing department, or from the health service – when the demand comes from a social worker or health visitor rather than from the poor themselves (Becker & Silburn 1990). The response is even more ready when the poor are portrayed as passive victims rather than as angry and defiant, and this further reinforces stereotypes of who are the deserving poor. While in the short term such practices may bring benefit to individual clients, in the longer term they do little to change the situation. On the contrary, as gatekeepers to restricted resources, welfare professionals need to take responsibility for the ways their actions might reinforce rather than challenge the powerlessness of the poor.

Professionals working with the poor need to decide if they are to be part of the problem or part of the solution. Recognising that they can be part of the problem, rather than simply accepting that what they do invariably benefits the poor, is an important first step. But welfare professionals have other responsibilities. Whether wittingly or unwittingly, the history of many welfare professions has been one of collusion in the great silence about poverty and in accepting the fragmentation of the poor into discrete client groups (Jones 1983). There is a need to challenge this compartmentalisation of the elderly, the disabled, single mothers, black people and other groups, and to begin to talk about and act upon the common experience of poverty which underlies many of the problems they are faced with.

If empowering the poor is to mean anything it must move away from representing the poor to mobilising the poor to take their own action. As Robert Chambers has argued:

> Deprivation and well-being have, then, many dimensions. Poor people have many priorities. What matters most to them often differs from what outsiders assume. If poor people's realities are to come first, development professionals have to be sensitive, to decentralise, and to empower, enabling poor people to conduct their own analysis and express their own multiple priorities (Chambers 1994 p10).

What this requires is the difficult task of mobilising the poor as poor. It means recognising and building upon the resources and strengths of poor people and communities, and overcoming the divisions that fragment them. Above all it calls for respect for the poor, and a willingness actively to listen to what they have to say

Empowerment and poverty
Of all the social and political movements that have flowered in Britain over the past three decades, and that have had a notion of empowerment as an essential part of their success, the poor have been largely noticeable for their absence. The civil rights and black power movement, the mobilisation of women, gay pride and activism and the challenge of disabled people, have all to a greater or lesser extent sought to confront stereotypes, to redefine identity, and to take strength and solidarity from a pride in their existence. Few people, and certainly within the economically developed societies of the world, take a pride, or even an identity, in being poor. On the contrary, the experience of generations for whom poverty has been stigmatised, in which dominant definitions and ideologies have gone largely unchallenged, and of an oppression that has had such damaging consequences, both physically and mentally, on millions of people has created a situation that most people seek simply to escape from or avoid.

The empowerment of the poor differs fundamentally from the empowerment of other social groups. For the ultimate aim of empowering the poor must be the eradication of poverty: an end to the poor, and not simply their acceptance into the social world from which they are frequently excluded. With this in mind, however, the means to doing so have many similarities. They require a questioning of how, and by whom, the poor are defined, a challenge to the images, caricatures and stereotypes through which poverty is presented, and a change in the way that the politics of poverty are mobilised. Increasingly, poverty has to be seen as an injustice rather than a misfortune, as a collective rather than an individual experience.

Challenging the dominant definitions and perceptions of poverty means also challenging the way that poverty and the poor are talked to and talked about. Discrimination against the poor is rife, pervasive and deep-rooted in our culture. Just as the anti-racist and women's movements have challenged stereotypes and the easy and unthinking use of derogatory language and images, so too there needs to be a greater awareness of the countless ways in which poor people are insulted, belittled and labelled in ways that reinforce a sense of powerlessness and oppression. The charge of political correctness that right-wing commentators have levelled against such efforts has been used to belittle this task, as if language were a neutral medium. Yet it is precisely the way that images of poverty and of the poor are constructed that needs to be challenged if empowerment is to have any meaning.

There is a need also to recognise the commonality of poverty. Both the threat and the experience of poverty are issues that affect not a small minority but a substantial part of the population. Almost two-thirds of the population of Britain live below the average level of income (DSS 1992 p1) and increasing numbers experience unprecedented levels of insecurity and the stress that goes with this. A campaign against poverty should not be seen as a minority appeal but as something of wide and popular benefit. The realisation of this situation is what makes the issue of poverty potentially such a politically explosive one, and the frustration of this potential can be seen in the many ways in which the poor are divided and set against each other.

Above all there is a need to recognise, work with and build upon the strengths, resources and capacities of poor people and communities (Lister & Beresford 1991). Poverty is a terribly destructive force: it saps people's health and energy, undermines self-confidence and feelings of self-worth, and puts immense strain on family and social relationships. Simply coping with the everyday realities of poverty is a hard enough struggle. The wonder is not so much why the poor have failed to realise their political potential, but how it is that not more are driven to self-destructive desperation, and how it is that the poor manage to survive and fight back.

Simply surviving poverty calls for skills and resources that belie many of the stereotypes ascribed to poor people. It frequently requires feats of organisation and budgetary skills that would defeat the abilities of the more affluent. It also calls upon reserves of solidarity, of generosity and mutual support that are all the more remarkable given the limited resources that poor people have to share. It is not necessary to romanticise poverty to recognise the extent to which poor people support each other, nor does it mean denying the conflicts and animosities that may arise. But the evidence of solidarity amongst the poor is a strength that needs to be recognised and built upon.

Equally important is the need to recognise that coping and survival are not the only features of poverty. To see them as such is to neglect the fact that the poor also have ambitions and aspirations (Jones 1993), that far from being enmeshed in a culture that accepts the inevitability of poverty there are many who seek to challenge and overcome it.

Poverty and Political Action
Political action against poverty is an awesome undertaking. Everything in society conspires against it – the lack of resources, the scale of the task, the debilitating effects of poverty itself, the disinterest if not the hostility of the major political parties and other social and political organisations, and the entrenched opposition and power of those who benefit from poverty and those who support them.

Occasionally, however, the poor revolt. Of all the political events in Britain over the past decade, the resistance to and eventual overthrow of the Poll Tax (and with it one of the twentieth century's most infamous political leaders) was one of huge significance and importance. This movement – although it acknowledged the support and contribution of those who 'Can Pay, Won't Pay' – was essentially a movement of those who 'Can't Pay, Won't Pay'. Despite the threat of legal sanction, despite the lack of support from the main opposition political parties, the poor in their millions stated that enough was enough. With a remarkable degree of organisation of community networks and support poor people mobilised to resist the actions of bailiffs, to set up avenues of communication, advice and help, to sustain opposition and so defy and ultimately defeat the State in what was one of the most widespread of civilian mobilisations in British history.

Less dramatically the struggles of the poor take on a more mundane, everyday but no less important character. They are both individual and collective, ranging from the ongoing skirmishes and battles with unsympathetic officials to community initiatives that prefigure very different forms of social organisation from dominant models of individualism and self-interest. Despite the undoubted difficulties, poor communities have organised a remarkable range of initiatives (see for example Community Development Journal 1995). Many of these reflect the need for survival: the organisation of credit unions, housing and other co-operatives, community employment initiatives, tenants' groups or of self-defence organisations against racist attacks. Others celebrate and build on the bonds of community, in festivals, galas, parties, music and drama. Yet more organise alternative educational provision or protest the actions of local government or the central state.

Many of these initiatives take place outside of – and sometimes in opposition to – the major political parties. Within countries like Britain there is developing a profound alienation from and distrust of the formal political process. From the point of view of the poor this is hardly surprising. Political reform within the structures of capitalist society has not solved the problems of poverty: fifty years of a welfare state have failed to create equality and in recent years have not managed to prevent a slide back to levels of inequality and polarisation unseen since the nineteenth century. Faith previously placed in the Labour Party as champions of the poor has proved unfounded. Whatever the reasons for this failure – and complex issues of political power, of the elusive nature of an increasingly international capitalism undoubtedly play a part – the Labour Party has forfeited its right to represent the poor. As it has moved increasingly to the Right, seeking to appeal to a narrow self-interest of middle income groups and espousing the values of the market that under its Conservative predecessors in government have done so much to increase poverty and deprivation, it has increased this sense of disillusionment.

This is perhaps no bad thing, although the political vacuum that is created risks the ever-present danger of fascism and right-wing totalitarianism. What is needed in its place is a new kind of politics and political struggle.

Empowerment is not something that can be done for the poor. Power has to be taken, and the taking of it is itself a process of empowerment: a gaining of confidence and of ability to control one's life. That poor people are capable of resisting, of organising to defend their interests, pursue their claims, and even to overthrow and reorder the society in which they live is a lesson both of history and of contemporary global developments that cannot be ignored. Such examples – and there are many – are a necessary corrective to the fatalism of those who see poverty as inevitable or the powers ranged against it as immune and untouchable. These lessons need to be learnt, and there is much to be learnt and much confidence to be gained by people in countries like Britain from the struggles of the poor in the Third World or the former Eastern bloc against totalitarian and oppressive regimes.

In the meantime, those who wish to help in this process need to begin by questioning their own assumptions and actions – by asking whose side they are on. From there, there is much work to do and many alliances to be formed. Poverty has to be got onto, and kept on, the political agenda. The invisibility and denial of poverty are one of the most potent weapons in the hands of those who benefit from it. It must constantly be exposed. Those whose work brings them into contact with poverty have at least a responsibility to speak out, and to counter the myths, deceits and lies that abound. They can also do much to help create alliances and break down those divisions that keep the poor fragmented, isolated and separate. Building barriers against poverty and the poor – as evidenced quite literally in the escalating growth of security measures, of locks, fences and patrols, or in attempts to build a 'Fortress Europe' against the poor of the rest of the world – is, as many people are coming to realise, simply no solution to the problem. Poverty disfigures the whole of society, and recognition of the need to do something about its causes rather than simply trying to suppress its consequences has the potential to unite many different groups.

The devaluation of the poor, their treatment as less than human beings, is an inevitable consequence of a society built upon gross inequalities of income, wealth and opportunity. To challenge this – by having respect for the poor, by acknowledging their experience and strengths, and learning from this – is a first and necessary step in challenging the ways in which such power and privilege are maintained.

References

Becker, S. and Silburn, R. (1990) *The New Poor Clients: Social Work,* Poverty and the Social Fund London, Community Care and the Benefits Research Unit.

Beresford, P. and Croft, S. (1995) Time for a new approach to anti-poverty campaigning *Poverty* 90.

Chambers, R. (1994) *Poverty and Livelihoods: Whose Reality Counts?* Paper prepared for the Stockholm Roundtable on Global Change 22-24 July 1994.

Community Development Journal (1995) Special issue. 'Perspectives on UK Community Work' Vol 30 No 2.

Dean, H. (1991). In search of the underclass. In P. Brown and R. Scase *Poor Work: Disadvantage and the Division of Labou*r. Milton Keynes, Open University Press.

Department of Social Security (1992) *Households Below Average Income: A Statistical Analysis* 1979-J988/9 HMSO.

Dobson, B. *et al* (1994) *Diet, Choice and Poverty: Social Cultural and Nutritional Aspects of Food Consumption Among Low-Income Families.* London, Family Policy Studies Centre.

Jones, C. (1983) *State Social Work and the Working Class* London, Macmillan.

Jones, D. (1993) The culture of achievement amongst the poor. *Critique of Anthropology* Vol 13 No 3.

Lister, R. & Beresford, P. (1991). *Working Together Against Poverty* Open Services Project.

Morris, L. (1994). *Dangerous Classes: The Underclass and Social Citizenship.* London, Routledge.

Novak, T. (1988) *Poverty and the State: An Historical Sociology.* Milton Keynes, Open University Press.

Novak, T. (1995) Re-thinking poverty. *Critical Social Policy* Vol 15 No 2.

Townsend, P. (1979) *Poverty in the United Kingdom.* Harmondsworth, Penguin.

Vincent, J. (1993) Framing the underclass. *Critique of Anthropology* Vol 13 No 3.

Chapter 7
Empowering Professionals in Higher Education?

Maureen Gillman

Introduction

It is difficult to imagine any form or model of education, or indeed any educator, that would not claim to have as a goal the 'empowerment' of students. The term 'empowerment' is used by a wide variety of theorists and practitioners to describe what might be seen as very contradictory practices. For example, empowerment in the context of education has been defined in the following terms as: self-actualisation, personal growth, skills acquisition, challenging power imbalances in the classroom, developing awareness of, and confronting discrimination and oppression in, education, collective action amongst disadvantaged groups, and a commitment to social justice and citizenship.

Some proponents of these approaches to empowerment see others' definitions as problematic. For example, Critical theorists who would support collective action and social justice perceive individualistic forms of empowerment as maintaining the *status quo* and rendering structural issues invisible (Avis 1991, Hodgkinson 1994). The new Right, on the other hand, would perceive a commitment to social justice in education as an obstacle to an individual's freedom of choice and action (Johnson 1991).

Empowerment of students is a claim that is made by a variety of educational approaches the belief systems and political orientations of which range from conservative forms of education characterised by technocracy and individualism, through the liberal tradition of critical thinking and self-actualisation to radical forms embodied in the notions of critical pedagogy. Baistow (1994) suggests that empowerment discourses across the political spectrum have common features; they see solutions as

'. . . being ground level, bottom-up, localised strategies to increase user choice, participation and the key theme, personal control' (p38).

Empowerment does not exist in a vacuum; it is a discursive practice which is informed and defined by the political, ideological and theoretical context of an educational programme. Power is not only central to the word emPOWERment but is also inextricably bound up with the relations between knowledge and education

Empowerment is sometimes spoken of as if it were in the gift of individuals. However, it is questionable whether individual educators are free to empower students given the constraints that might be found in any educational programme. For example: the institutionalised discrimination found at every level of education in our society; the normative and 'conformative' nature of many training programmes; the disciplinary power invested in the restrictions of content of course curricula; and the forms of assessment of competence imposed by professional bodies and/or institutions of education and training. See also Green, Martin and Williams (this volume.)

Some writers in the field of professional education and training have begun to question the utility of the concept of empowerment to explain the relations between students and their educational programmes. Rossiter (1993), writing about social work education, suggests that the term 'empowerment' has become 'a part of a rhetoric at the expense of retaining substantive meaning' (p81). McWilliam (1992) describes empowerment in teacher education as 'a pedagogy of good intentions' (p.14).

There exists within the context of professional education and training a tension between, on the one hand, the need to train students to act effectively within the dominant paradigms and values of the profession and on the other the desire to encourage students to be critical thinkers and reflective practitioners. The remainder of this chapter will examine the relations of domination and 'empowerment' in the management of such tensions.

Professional power/knowledge
The liberal, humanist paradigm in education assumes that knowledge is distinct from power. Power is seen as coercive and repressive whilst knowledge is perceived as liberating (Edwards and Usher 1994). Foucault (1980, 1988) challenged this paradigm by suggesting that power and knowledge are inseparable from one another. They are 'regimes of truth' (Foucault 1988) through which knowledge practices, discourses and techniques are manifested and power exercised. Critical pedagogues perceive education as a form of 'cultural politics' where relations of domination are produced and maintained through the power of knowledge (Rossiter 1993 p.77).

Professional 'disciplines' have developed knowledge discourses which allow them to specify certain 'truths' about the world of those who consult them. Rossiter (1993) writing about social work training suggests that 'we listen to our clients' voices through theoretical filters generated within political relations.' (p78). As 'knowledgeable experts', professionals' opinions, derived from the application of their theories and paradigms, are perceived to be rational, neutral and respectable (White 1993).

Professional discourses afford the statements of professionals the status of truth because they uphold the dominant discourses in society. For example, Hare Mustin (1994) suggests that family therapists are well regarded in society because they support dominant discourses such as maintaining families and keeping children in school. Professional knowledge and theories and their discursive practices 'discipline' individuals and reproduce 'acceptable' subjects who conform to dominant societal beliefs and behaviour.

Dominant political ideology is reflected in the discourses of individualism, consumerism, citizenship and market forces, which have been strongly influential in the 1980s and 1990s. Social policies which directly affect the welfare professions and their clients/patients are underpinned by notions of individual responsibility, individual rights and survival of the fittest. For example, all 'social' explanations for societal problems, such as crime or unemployment, have been redefined as personal troubles and individual culpability.

These dominant discourses are reflected in professional knowledge, theories and paradigms which are concerned with personal growth, self-actualisation, and overcoming personal' adversity in order to measure up to the norm. These include such knowledge discourses as psychotherapy, counselling, cognitive therapy, groupwork, normalisation principles, and behaviour modification. Concentrating on the individual as the target for change renders invisible structural issues such as poverty, race, class, gender and disabling barriers in society.

The exercise of disciplinary power in the context of professional training
Professionals are subject to disciplinary power through the discourses that dominate the systems of their education and training. 'Professional' educators exercise their disciplinary power when they use paradigms and theories of education and learning to construct a process of training for students.

Edwards and Usher (1994) argue that in the present economic and political climate, 'knowledge based' vocational qualifications have been seen to have failed the expectations of employers who have criticised them on the grounds of lack of fitness for purpose. There has been a shift towards a discourse of competence in which knowledge and understanding is assumed in the skilled technical performance of competencies. The notion of competence has become increasingly embedded in the discourses of vocational and professional education. For example, changes in social work education embodied in the DipSW (CCETSW 1989), include a more 'practical', skills-based training, jointly designed and provided by partnerships of employers and educational institutions. Another, more recent example is the reforms to teacher training which maintain that

> '. . . training should take place in schools rather than institutes of higher education, it should be practical rather than theoretical, and the success or failure of trainees should depend upon their performance against a detailed list of competencies that can be demonstrated as having been achieved'
> Hall and Millard (1994 p153).

In some quarters, competence-based learning is perceived as progressive and empowering. Edwards and Usher (1994) assert that it is so perceived because of its use of humanist language and practices such as

> 'student centred learning, negotiating of individual learning programmes, the accreditation of prior learning. . . It is precisely through its articulation with liberal, humanist ideas that discourses of competence are powerful, not simply with the formal structures of education and training but, more important, over and through learners' (p9).

The strongly held beliefs of educators about ideologies of teaching and learning and their related preferences for content of course curricula are embodied in their exercise of disciplinary power. McWilliam (1992) argues that 'regimes of truth' contained in the educational ideologies and discursive practices of educators may render students passive. Students 'oppositional voices' may well be marginalised or silenced by educators' assumptions that they know what is good for students.

McWilliam (1992) cites Smith and Zantiotis (1988), who identified two discursive traditions within the field of teacher education. The 'dominant' discourse is characterised by a technocratic approach to teacher education in which the trainer is the expert and the trainee the apprentice. Teacher training is aimed at effectiveness and competence that will 'fit the requirements of an emerging economic order' (p77). The *'avant garde'* discourse is identified as being anchored in the concepts of emancipation, liberation and democracy. It seeks to problematise the dominant discourse and its context of structural oppression by calling for curricula which focus on social justice. The *avant garde* discourse is said to he a reaction to the perceived 'disempowering' nature of the dominant discourse and its proponents claim to have as their goal the empowerment and emancipation of students.

Similar *'avant garde'* approaches to professional training exist in many disciplines including social work (Rossiter 1993, de Maria 1992), medicine (Haas and Shaffir 1982), and family therapy (Hoffman 1990, Atkinson and Heath 1990). In the late 1980s and early 1990s family therapy trainers have written about the development of *avant garde* approaches to training which they refer to as 'second order' (Anderson and Rambo 1988, White 1989, Anderson and Swim 1993). For example, Kazan *et al* (1993) suggest that, in their programme, a deconstructive approach is combined with a narrative metaphor in which trainee therapists are encouraged to

'. . . examine their own history and training in order to discover unique outcomes from their lives and thus construct a new story about their skills and strengths as therapists' (p201).

They add that training focuses, in particular, on the dominant fields of power/knowledge that affect the field of family therapy. In addition, trainees are encouraged to develop their own unique style of therapy, 'not to try and slavishly imitate the trainer/therapist' (p204).

Anderson and Swim (1993) suggest that their training programme is underpinned by a philosophy of learning as a collaborative and egalitarian effort, in which learners are considered expert in their understanding of themselves and their clients. 'They are responsible, along with teachers and other learners, for determining the agenda, goals and strategy of the learning process' (p145). They add that the trainers' 'philosophical bias' informs the learning process and the roles of the participants.

Whilst learners are encouraged to question theories and practices offered by participants in the course, it does not appear to be acceptable for trainees to question the programme's 'philosophical bias'. Anderson and Swim (1993) state that many students begin the programme with a need and an expectation to be advised what to do by trainers who hold expertise in family therapy. They suggest that such requests 'dissolve' as participants become 'active architects of their own learning' (p150).

As in dominant or 'first order' models of family therapy training, students are immersed in the language practices of the dominant discourses (or trainers' philosophical biases). In both models of training, students are deemed to have reached their learning goals when they are able to use the language of the dominant discourse. For example, Anderson and Swim (1993) argue that students and trainers are interdependent and contribute, in conversation, to the development of new knowledge. However:

'. . . it is apparent from the [learner's] use of words such as 'conversation', listening' and 'dialogue', and of phrases such as 'development of new meaning' that she learned these from the programme' (p150).

It is here at the level of learning process that students are inducted into the dominant discourses of hermeneutics and social constructionism etc. At this level of 'empowering' educational practice, such concepts are not open to question. Such 'empowering' practices are isomorphically and dialogically translated into the content and process of trainees' practice with families. Family therapy trainees are not only learning about family therapy, they are also learning the subtleties of empowerment practices through their subjugation to disciplinary power.

McWilliam (1992) suggests that students' 'oppositional voices' critique the *avant garde* as well as the dominant discourse. Criticism of the *avant garde* is based on such issues as the students' needs for skills, which are, in turn, framed by *avant garde* educators as 'latent conservatism'. She suggests that educators should critique their own impositional tendencies and models of emancipatory practice.

'Educators should acknowledge the difference between the need for understanding advocacy teaching and actually doing it. Student teachers certainly understand the difference because they are often forced to live it out in very disempowering ways' (McWilliam 1992 p15).

However morally or politically correct an educational approach may be, there is no escape from the practices of disciplinary power.

'. . . there can be no such thing as an asocial or presocial autonomous subject; to be subject is to be discursively constituted and subject to disciplinary power. There is nowhere where subjects are not already in discourse, or where they can be completely untouched by power/knowledge formations' (Edwards and Usher 1994 p3).

Technologies of power
The practices of power in professional education are built into bodies of knowledge where they represent respectable regimes of truth. Foucault (1977) asserted that the 'disciplines' characterise, classify and hierarchise individuals in relation to one another and, if necessary, disqualify and invalidate. Such disciplinary power is exercised in education through the practices of observation and surveillance. It takes the form of assessment procedures and appraisal mechanisms in which subjects are classified by their capacity to meet normative standards and 'objective' criteria. Subjects become 'objects' of surveillance when such procedures are exercised. Foucault argued that:

'A relation of surveillance, defined and regulated, is inscribed at the heart of the practice of teaching, not as an additional or adjacent part, but as a mechanism that is inherent to it and increases its efficiency' (cited in Edwards and Usher 1994 p.5).

The content and expected outcome of professional training are dictated by professional bodies and dominant societal discourses. Students on professional training courses are expected to demonstrate their adherence to dominant professional discourses and values. Such adherence is encouraged through the technologies of power built into systems of assessment and evaluation. Rossiter (1993) argued that social work education creates products rather than persons. 'With a product rather than a person at the centre of the educational project, the possibility of empowerment is diminished' (p82). Similarly, Su (1990) found that the product of professional socialisation for teachers was a reproduction of the stereotyped teacher and 'a perpetuation of the existing culture of teaching and schooling' (p386).

In many professional education contexts supervision of practice is a major part of the training and can also be perceived as a technology of power. Light (1980), who studied the professional training of psychiatrists, asserted that group supervision was the major agent of socialisation in that it greatly increased the students' investment and commitment and 'made them dependent on professional models' (p261). Similarly, writers in the field of social work training have argued that supervised practice placements are the most significant part of training a student to take on board the 'mantle' of social work (Gardiner 1989, Holland 1989).

In my own research into family therapy training (Gillman 1994) 'live supervision' was found to be not only an integral part of the training but also central to the discipline of family therapy itself (Burnham 1986, Haley 1993). Live supervision is the observation of a therapist working with a family, through the medium of a one-way mirror or closed-circuit TV system. The role of the (live) supervision group is to maintain a 'meta' position to the family-plus-therapist system, and to comment on, or direct interactions within, that system (Hoffman 1981).

Acting as the mouthpiece of the supervision group had a number of major consequences for the students. It was seductive in that it gave the students a taste of success and therefore increased motivation to learn more; it increased dependence and enmeshment of the student with their supervision group; it promoted the tutor as 'expert' and someone to emulate; and it increased peer group pressure to conform the new model on offer (Gillman 1994).

Luepnitz (1992) suggested that Foucault's ideas about surveillance could inform a critique of the one-way mirror in family therapy. Foucault (1977) used the analogy of Jeremy Bentham's panoptican to describe the dominant culture's control of subjects by observation. Bentham laid down the principle that power should be visible and unverifiable.

Clinical family therapy can be perceived as the surveillance, control and reshaping of 'dysfunctional' or deviant families. The unseen observers behind the one-way screen are sometimes perceived by the family and the therapist as intimidating. Such arrangements have been found to encourage conformity and acquiescence in both the family and the trainee therapist. Live-supervision can be viewed as a form of panopticism in the contexts of therapy and training. For the students undertaking family therapy training in my research, live-supervision appeared to represent a shared ordeal, which united the students in an interdependent and supportive relationship with each other and the course staff. In order to pass the course, a student's commitment to family therapy had to be demonstrated through observed, supervised and evaluated practice. Under these technologies of power, it was difficult for a 'doubting' student to pass as a 'believer' (Gillman 1994).

Light (1980) referred to a process of 'false consciousness' in which the student, in order to negotiate her own socialisation, . . . must understand the terms of one's mentors, and use the language,symbols and paradigms of the profession. Then the process itself immerses one even more and teaches one the refinements, which in themselves take for granted what was doubted or challenged' (p311).

Role playing and negotiating more influence in the supervision group were found to immerse the student in the 'culture' of the Family Therapy Course and the professional discipline. The students were seduced by their very attempts to construct their resistance (Gillman 1994).

Edwards and Usher (1994) suggest that surveillance does not necessarily mean the direct gaze of the lecturer/trainer. Other forms of 'observation' include continuous assessment and peer evaluation. Whilst such forms of evaluation are usually introduced in order to liberate students from formal examinations and hierarchical assessment, students do not necessarily experience such strategies as liberating or empowering.

Haas and Shaffir (1982) observed medical students undertaking a programme of medical training that is described by the authors as somewhat unusual in its pedagogical approach. The programme was based upon the notions of self-directed learning and problem solving. One feature of the course was peer group evaluation, rather than formal examination or 'faculty evaluation'. The authors found that students experienced peer group evaluation as oppressive for a number of reasons. The students felt as if they were constantly under scrutiny whilst also feeling obliged to make judgements on others. Students worried about posing a threat to another student and the possible 'tit for tat' repercussions of criticising progress of another student. Students felt that the peer evaluation was essentially a 'verbal' system in which those who were confident and competent in such an arena were able to project a better image of professionalism. Haas and Shaffir (1982) concluded that:

'The innovative professional setting that we studied differs in curriculum and pedagogical methods from traditional medical schools. Yet these differences do not seem to alter the character of ritual ordeal that students experience. In both settings, students must accommodate themselves to uncertainty' (p149).

Professional socialisation and technologies of the self
From a functionalist perspective, professional socialisation involves the induction of recruits into a common core of homogenous beliefs and norms (Schuval and Adler 1980). The students are seen as passive recipients who are acted upon by teachers who have the power to initiate them into a shared-belief system. Students are involved in a process of 'role learning' and 'situational adjustment' in which individual characteristics and experience play little or no part.

This view has been criticised by a number of writers who have suggested that students play an active part in the construction of their own socialisation (Bucher and Strauss 1961, Light 1980, Forsyth and Danisiewicz 1985). However, Light (1980), who researched the socialisation of psychiatrists, suggested that despite the active participation of students in the construction of their professional identity, they turn out alike in those aspects which their mentors deem essential (p309).

Foucault (1980) put forward the view that modern power is not negative or restrictive hut positive and 'constitutive'. He suggested that practices of power regulate and form subjects through a process of self-regulation and self-discipline. Foucault referred to such constitutive power as

'... technologies of the self, which permit individuals to effect by their own means, or with the help of others, a certain number of operations on their own bodies and souls, thoughts, conduct and way of being, so as to transform themselves in order to attain a certain state of happiness, purity, wisdom or immortality' (1980 p18).

White (1993) suggested that modern power is decentralised and 'taken up' rather than being centralised and exercised from the top down. Foucault suggested that subjects collaborate in the policing of their own lives. Individuals do not see such power practices as negative or repressive but as fulfilling and liberating. For example, in my own research into family therapy training (Gillman 1994), it was evident that students came on the course expecting to be encouraged to 'unlearn' practices perceived to be in conflict with family therapy; to refrain from questioning the new learning on offer; and to feel deskilled during the training. Such experiences were perceived by the students as an essential part of becoming a family therapist. Practices of power embedded in the discourses of family therapy, such as the peer group and self surveillance associated with live-supervision, recruited students as willing subjects in the disciplining of their own subjugation.

Empowerment as a professional theory of practice

In the 1980s and 1990s, empowerment has become a central theme and a body of knowledge for professional practice in the welfare professions (Baistow 1994, Ward and Mullender 1991, Rose and Black 1985, Adams 1990). Baistow (1994) argues that those who 'do the empowering' are likely to be social workers, health visitors, nurses, clinical psychologists and psychotherapists (p37). Professionals' claims to empowerment as a knowledge base places them at the centre of empowering activity, where they assume the right to determine the needs of those to be empowered (Rose and Black 1985) and to apply the technologies of practice to bring about empowerment (Swift and Levin 1987).

The professionalisation of empowerment can be seen as a reaction to the development of new social movements in the 80s and 90s. These include user involvement, self-help groups such as women's, black and gay and lesbian organisations, and the disability movement. Such movements have challenged the notion of expert, professional knowledge and the provision of professionally designed services (Croft and Beresford 1992). There are now many examples of user-designed and user-led services, which celebrate the knowledge and expertise of users to define and meet their own needs (French 1994).

Such developments may be liberatory for users but they may also threaten the elitist power/knowledge and status of those professionals who claim exclusive rights to such areas of practice. However, as empowerment is seen as an ethically

worthy exercise and a moral imperative (Stevenson and Parsloe 1993), professionals have adopted a 'meta' position in which they claim to be the experts in the
definition and operation of empowerment practice.

Rossiter (1993) argues that both social work practitioners and educators do not see
social work knowledge as problematic. She argues that social work knowledge
should be treated as 'an artefact of a culture organised in terms of relations of
domination' (p78).

Whilst professional theories of empowerment might appear, on the surface, to be
anti-discriminatory and anti-oppressive, it is necessary for this particular body of
knowledge (along with other professional knowledge bases) to be treated as problematic in its potential for oppression. Baistow (1994) argues that if
empowerment is a professional imperative, then there are dangers for those users
who either decide to empower themselves or refuse to be empowered at all (p.41).
A salutary example can be found in the exposition of normalisation theory (now
known as 'social role valorisation' (Wolfensberger 1984). Croft and Beresford
(1992) argue that the theory of normalisation offers a coherent value base and a
participatory framework (p.31). However, Wolfensberger argues that a socially
valued role can be imposed upon a user if the user does not respond to persuasion
or education.

> 'First, one pursues the line of persuasion, pedagogy, modelling and other
> forms of culturally normative social influences to steer a person toward a
> course of action one desires. Second, one imposes coercion only where one
> would do so legally in the larger societal context . . . Third, one chooses the
> least restrictive alternative if one does coerce' (Wolfensberger 1984 p1 10).

Isomorphisms between professional training and practice
Several authors have commented upon the isomorphisms between professional
training and practice (Ward and Mullender 1991, Bor 1989, Elizur 1990, Haley
1993). Hofstadter (1980) suggests that the term 'isomorphism' applies:

> '. . . when two complex structures can be mapped onto each other, in such a
> way that to each part of the structure there is a corresponding part in the
> other structure where 'corresponding' means that the two parts play similar
> roles in their respective structures' (p49).

This process is clearly illustrated in the processes of family therapy training and
practice (Gillman 1994). For example, comparisons can be made between the
interventions of a therapist with a family and the intervention of the live-supervision team with the trainee family therapist. Whilst the therapist tries to promote

change in a dysfunctional family by changing the family's view of the problem, the live supervision team is also attempting to change the therapist's linear perspective to that of a 'systemic' view.

Another striking similarity between therapy and training can be found in such routine therapeutic strategies as 'task-setting' and 'rituals', on the one hand, and team directives and 'prescriptions' on the other. Families are often expected to perform rituals and tasks as 'homework' after clinical family therapy sessions. Families are not usually provided with rationales for the tasks but asked to 'trust' the therapist's expert judgement that the task/ritual will be worthwhile. Similarly, trainee therapists are often given messages/prescriptions by the supervision team which they are expected to deliver to the family, often without the trainees being provided with the rationales for such interventions. In both cases, a 'conditioned' response is required, based on trust and 'faith' between the family and the trainee, and between the trainee and the live supervision team.

Isomorphisms can also be found in the epistemologies that inform, on the one hand, models of teaching and learning in professional training, and on the other, theories and paradigms of practice. One example is educational models which Freire (1981) refers to as 'banking approaches', where students become the depositories and teachers the depositors. Students passively receive the deposits and then memorise and reproduce them. The epistemology which underpins such educational approaches also underpins models of practice which assume that it is possible to influence a client/user by the use of this or that technique 'I programme you; I teach you; I instruct you' (Hoffman 1990 p5). In both situations, (teaching and practice) the individual becomes over-invested in producing specific changes in the student/client and over-committed in their belief in the efficacy of their techniques to produce a 'predictable outcome'.

Similarly, isomorphisms can be traced in the teaching and practice of more avant garde approaches, namely those associated with the notion of challenging oppression and sharing power. For example, educational theorists such as Shor and Freire (1987) and Giroux (1983, 1991) suggest that empowerment is a key concept in the reformulation of power imbalances between educators and students. They propose various strategies for sharing and redistributing power, such as providing students with the analytical skills to make objective and rational decisions about the merits, or otherwise, of knowledge discourses; portraying the teacher as learner of the student's reality; and opening up for debate the inevitability of the directiveness and authoritarianism of education. Ellsworth (1989) argues that critical pedagogues see the purpose of their efforts as 'empowerment for human betterment . . . and the capacity to act effectively' (p307).

Again, empowerment has become increasingly central to the practice of workers in the welfare professions (Baistow 1994). Ward and Mullender (1991) argue that there is an urgent need to fill the vacuum of empowering activity in the mainstream of professional social work practice. Strategies such as the relinquishment of professional power to clients associated with the self-help and user movements (Adams 1990); combining workers efforts with those of oppressed groups, without colonising them (Ward and Mullender 1991); and increasing consumer choice and individual potential for personal growth. In avant garde approaches to teaching and practice there are a number of assumptions, namely that empowerment is good for you, that such approaches have the political and moral high ground and are therefore progressive and unproblematic.

The problematics of empowerment in professional education
The concept of empowerment in the context of professional education (and practice) needs to be regarded as problematic for a number of reasons. There is a need for the high moral overtones and liberatory discourses of empowerment to be deconstructed in relation to the dominant political ideology. The rise of the concept of empowerment needs to be understood in the context of the ongoing attacks upon the welfare state; the attempts to reduce the status and power of professionals; and the growing domination of market forces in higher education.

The 1980s and early 1990s have been a time of considerable change in higher education in Britain. Changes in the philosophy, structure and organisation have been influenced by the prevailing political climate of consumerism, market forces and financial constraint upon the public sector (Williams 1991). Policy reforms and legislative changes, such as the 'Education Reform Act' 1988, have brought about major changes in governance in higher education. For example, the control of polytechnics was removed from local education authorities and two new national funding councils were established (Stubbs 1991). Pratt and Silverman (1988) put forward the view that the reforms represented an increase in central control over higher education which ensured adherence to government policies such as 'enterprise'.

Such adherence to government policies is evident in the development of 'National Vocational Qualifications' and 'Enterprise in Higher Education' which moved attention away from input measures as a means of assessing quality of programmes and brought 'outcomes' more sharply into focus (Ball 1991 p105). The debates about 'quality' in higher education in the l980s and early 90s widened the definition of the concept to include the 'quality' of learning outcomes and their 'fitness for purpose' (Williams and Loder 1990 p.2).

New partnership arrangements with employers have opened up the debates about the 'proper aims' of higher education; quality is indicated by student achievement including their acceptability to employers (Wright 1990, Perry 1991). The emphasis upon skill acquisition and competency embodied in the reforms of the 80s and 90s has stimulated the development of teaching and learning strategies which require more active forms of student centred approaches (Blackstone 1991).

The notion of empowerment in the field of education and training gives the somewhat erroneous impression that the institutionalised discrimination and oppression found in educational institutions is capable of being 'solved' by the use of empowering strategies. The use of such techniques pays lip-service to the notion of equality whilst leaving the authoritarian nature of the teacher/student relationship intact and the paternalistic nature of education unproblematised (Ellsworth 1989).

Empowerment seems to have a somewhat 'Janus-like' quality in that it can appear to be both radical and conservative and is, indeed, claimed by those at both ends of the political spectrum. Whilst masquerading as a radical and anti-oppressive practice in the hands of the welfare professions, it also embraces dominant ideologies of personal achievement and individual responsibility where the goals of empowerment are to enable individuals to take responsibility for themselves. Empowerment failures such as lack of employment or some forms of ill health are seen as the result of personal shortcomings, such as failure to achieve suitable qualifications or indulging in practices which are known to be a risk to health, such as smoking.

As discussed earlier in this chapter, empowerment has become a theory of professional practice in which professionals have taken up a central role in defining need and developing the technologies of empowerment. Similar developments can be seen in the context of education where empowerment is characterised by such developments as student-centred and self-directed learning (McKenzie, O'Reilly and Stephenson 1985, Birch 1986, Taylor 1986). Whilst these practices give the impression of more student autonomy, professional educators continue to theorise around these developments and create models and structures, such as Enquiry

Action Learning (Burgess and Jackson 1990), in which they are central and meta to the resources and techniques required to facilitate student learning. The adoption of more humanistic and egalitarian approaches towards teaching and learning does not necessarily signify the decline of the exercise of power. Marshall (1989) suggests that such developments represent

'. . . more subtle refinements of technologies of power based upon knowledge which has itself been produced within or used by the discipline of education. This knowledge, constituted in practice, comes in turn to legitimate practice' (p 108).

In the context of professional education and training, educators not only practise empowerment techniques but also teach them. Empowerment 'theory' validates and is validated by the contexts of education and practice. Domination and empowerment in professional socialisation are not necessarily at opposite ends of a continuum; it is possible to view empowerment as a more subtle refinement of domination, cloaked in the respectability of liberatory discourse.

References
Adams, R. (1990) *Self Help, Social Work and Empowerment.* MacMillan Education.

Anderson, N.H. and Rambo, A. (1988) An experiment in family therapy training: a trainer and trainee perspective. *Journal of Strategic and Systemic Therapies* 7, 54 - 70.

Anderson, H. and Swim, S. (1993) Learning as collaborative conversation: combining the student's and the teacher's expertise. *Human Systems* 4, 145 - 153.

Atkinson, B. J. and Heath, A.W. (1990) Further thoughts on second-order family therapy: this time it's personal. *Family Process* 29, 145 - 155.

Avis, J. (1991) Educational Practice, Professionalism and Social Relations. [In] *Education Group 11, Education Limited: Schooling and Training and the New Right Since 1979.* Unwin.

Baistow, K. (1994) Liberation and regulation? Some paradoxes of empowerment. *Critical Social Policy* 42, 34-46.

Ball, C. (1991) Quality and Qualities: an Overview. In T. Schuller (ed) *The Future of Higher Education.* SRHE and OU Press.

Birch, W. (1986) Towards a model for problem-based learning. *Studies in Higher Education* 13, 73 - 82.

Blackstone, T. (1991) Access, Quality and Governance. One Institution's Struggle for Progress. In T. Schuller (ed) *The Future of Higher Education.* SRHE and OU Press.

Bor, R. (1989) Teaching and learning a systems approach to family therapy: a theoretical review. *Issues in Social Work Education* 9, 31 - 36.

Bucher, R., Strauss, A. L. (1961) Professions in process *American Journal of Sociology* 66, 325 - 334.

Burgess, H. and Jackson, S. (1990) Enquiry and action learning: a new approach to social work education. *Social Work Education* 9, 3 - 19.

Burnham, J. (1986) *Family Therapy*. Tavistock Publications.

CCETSW (1989) Paper 30 *Dip S W - Requirements and Regulations for the Diploma in Social Work*. London: CCETSW.

Croft, S. and Beresford, P. (1992) The politics of participation. *Critical Social Policy* 35, 20-44.

de Maria, W. (1992) On the trail of a radical pedagogy for social work education. *British Journal of Social Work* 22, 231 - 252.

Department of Education(1988) *The Education Reform Act*. London HMSO.

Edwards, R. and Usher, R. (1994) Disciplining the subject: the power of competence. *Studies in the Education of Adults* 26, 1 - 14.

Elizur, J. (1990) Stuckness in live supervision: extending the therapist's style. *Journal of Family Therapy* 12, 267 - 280.

Ellsworth, E. (1989) Why doesn't this feel empowering? Working through the repressive myths of critical pedagogy. *Harvard Educational Review* 39, 297 - 323.

Forsyth, P B.; Danisiewicz T. J (1985) Towards a theory of professionalization. *Work and Occupations* 12, 59 - 76.

Foucault, M. (1977) *Discipline and Punish*. Penguin Books.

Foucault, M. (1980) *Power/knowledge: Selected Interviews and Other Writings*. Harvester Press.

Foucault, M. (1988) Technologies of the Self. [In] L. H Martin, H. Gutman and P H. Hutton (eds) *Technologies of the Self*. Tavistock Publications.

Freire, P. (1981) *Pedagogy of the Oppressed*. New York: Continuum.

French, S. (ed) (1994) *On Equal Terms: working with disabled people*. Butterworth - Heinemann Ltd.

Gardiner, D. W. (1989) Improving students' learning - setting an agenda for quality in the 1990s. *Issues in Social Work Education* 8, 3 - 10.

Gillman, M. A. (1994) *'Learning to Think Systemically': The Impact of Systemic Training upon Professionals and their Working Lives*. Thesis submitted for the award of Ph.D. University of Northumbria at Newcastle.

Giroux, H. A. (1983) *Theory and Resistance in Education: a pedagogy for the opposition*. Heinemann Educational Books.

Giroux, H. A.(ed) (1991) *Postmodernism, Feminism and Cultural Politics: redrawing educational boundaries*. State University of New York Press.

Haas, J. and Shaffir, W. (1982) Ritual evaluation of competence: the hidden curriculum of professionalization in an innovative medical school program. *Work and Occupations* 9, 131 - 154.

Haley, J. (1993) How to be a therapy supervisor without knowing how to change anyone. *Journal. of Systemic Therapies* 12.

Hall, C. and Millard, E. (1994) The means of correct training? Teachers, Foucault and disciplining. *Journal of Education for Teaching* 20, 153 - 160.

Hare Mustin, R. T. (1994) Discourses in the mirrored room: a postmodern analysis of therapy. *Family Process* 13, 19 - 35.

Hodgkinson, N. P. (1994) Empowerment as an entitlement in the post-16 curriculum. *Journal of Curriculum Studies* 25, 491 - 508.

Hoffman, L. (1981) *Foundations of Family Therapy* Basic Books Inc.

Hoffman, L. (1990) Constructing realities: an art of lenses. *Family Process* 29, 1 - 12.

Hofstadter, D. R. (1980) *Godel, Escher and Bach: an eternal Golden Braid.* Basic Books.

Holland, R. (1989) Visible and invisible curricula in professional education. *Issues in Social Work Education* 8-9, 83 - III

Johnson. R. (1991) My new right education. [In) *Education Group 11, Education limited: schooling and training and the new right since 1979*. Unwin-Hyman.

Kazan, Z.; Anderson, L.; Law, L. and Swan, V. (1993) *Narrative therapy, deconstruction and training. Human Systems* 4, 201 - 206.

Light, D. (1980) *Becoming Psychiatrists*. W.W. Norton.

Luepnitz, D. A. (1992) Nothing in common but their first names: the case of Foucault and White. *Journal of Family Therapy* 14,281 - 284.

Marshall, J. (1989) Foucault and Education. *Australian Journal. Of Education* 33,2.

McKenzie, E. J.; O'Reilly, D. and Stephenson, J. (1985) Independent study and professional education. *Studies in Higher Education* 10, 187 - 198.

McWilliam, E. (1992) Towards advocacy: post-positivist directions for progressive teacher educators. *British Journal of Sociology Of Education* 13, 3 - 17.

Perry, P. (1991) Quality in Higher Education. In T. Schuller (ed) *The Future of Higher Education*. SRHE and OU Press.

Pratt, J. and Silverman S. (1988) Responding to Constraint: Policy and Management in Higher Education. SRHE and OU Press.

Rose, S. M. and Black, B. L. (1985) *Advocacy and Empowerment: mental health care in the community*. RKP.

Rossiter, A. B. (1993) Teaching from a critical perspective: towards empowerment in social work education. *Canadian Social Work Review* 10, 76 - 90.

Schuval, J. T. and Adler, I. (1980) The role of models in professional socialization. *Social Science Med.* 14a, 8 - 14.

Shor, I. and Freire, P. (1987) *A Pedagogy for Liberation: dialogues on transforming education*. Bergin and Garvey.

Smith, R. and Zantiotis, A. (1988) Practical teacher education and the avant garde. *Journal of Curriculum Theorizing* 8, 77 - 106.

Stevenson, O. and Parsloe, P. (1993) *Community Care and Empowerment*. Joseph Rowntree Foundation.

Stubbs, W. H. (1991) Governance and Sectoral Differentiation. In T. Schuller (ed) *The Future of Higher Education* SRHE and OU Press.

Su, Z. (1990) Exploring the moral socialisation of teacher candidates (1). *Oxford Review Of Education* 16,367 - 391.

Swift, C. and Leving, G. (1987) Empowerment: an emerging mental health technology. *Journal. of Primary Prevention* 8.

Taylor, M. (1986) Learning for self-direction in the classroom: the pattern of a transition process. *Studies in Higher Education* 11, 55 72.

Ward, D. and Mullender, A. (1991) Empowerment and oppression: an indissoluble pairing for contemporary social work. *Critical Social Policy* 32,21 - 30.

White, M. (1989) Family therapy training and supervision in a world of experience and narrative. *Dulwich Centre Newsletter* Summer 1989/90.

White, M. (1993) Deconstruction and therapy. [In] S. Gilligan and R Price (eds) Therapeutic Conversations. W.W. Norton.

Williams, G. (1991) Finished and Unfinished Business. In T. Schuller (ed) *The Future of Higher Education*. SRHE and OU Press.

Williams, G. and Loder. C. P. J. (1990) The Importance of Quality and Quality Assurance. In C. P. J. Loder (ed) *Quality Assurance and Accountability in Higher Education*. Institute of Education. University of London.

Wolfensburger, W. (1984) A reconceptualization of normalization as social role valorization. *Mental Retardation* 34, 22 - 25.

Wright, P. (1990) Strategic Change in the Higher Education Curriculum: The example of the Enterprise in Higher Education Initiative, , C. P J Loder *op. cit.*

Chapter 8
Critical Consciousness or Commercial Consciousness?
Dilemmas in Higher Education

Mary Green, Marion Martin and Jan Williams

Introduction

Is it realistic to continue to work towards empowering approaches to education in the increasingly narrow, instrumentalist context of higher education in the UK today? Our intention in this chapter is to explore this question, focusing our discussion on a case study of a Masters Course in Education for Primary Health Care (EPHC) which two of the authors co-ordinate. In the first part of the chapter we describe the course, its objectives, and some of the problems associated with critical education (CE). In the second section we examine the institutional and political climate in which the course operates.

The Education for Primary Health Care course

On the EPHC course we seek to offer an international learning forum for health-related professionals, to better equip them for their development work in primary health care settings. The majority of course participants have considerable experience in their own professional fields. The course offers them the opportunity to reflect critically on their experiences in the light of theoretical perspectives which emphasise a people-centred philosophy of health and development (Sanders 1985). The educational theories Paulo Freire (Freire 1972) strongly influence the methodology adopted. Issues of inequality, particularly those of gender, are central to the curriculum and our approach to adult education. International and critical feminist perspectives such as those represented in the work of feminists like Vandana Shiva and Maria Mies (1993), Chandra Mohanty (1991) and Lesley Doyal (1995) play a central role in influencing the theoretical framework that shapes the course. The explicit political bias of course content towards the marginalised in society is given mandate by the Alma Ata Declaration of PHC (WHO 1978), which recognises inequity of access to health by disenfranchised groups and aims to redress this balance.

Informed by these theoretical positions we aim to facilitate an understanding of health and development which takes on board diverse historical, political, cultural and international perspectives. We seek to do this through educational processes that emphasise participatory/experiential learning methods and stimulate critical reflection. The aim is to facilitate the capacity for the learner group to develop strategies to create positive change in their lives, work and communities.

The EPHC course runs over one year full time or two to five years part time: the great majority of our students are full time, which means that group-oriented education and assessment processes are possible. This suits our educational goal of facilitating critical approaches to education. The course consists of eight modules, a module being made up of a number of taught units on a particular subject, assessed at the end of the module. Assessments take the form of essays and group project work. Four of the modules are in PHC subjects and two are options. The remaining two make up the dissertation.

Course participants range in age from about twenty-five to forty-five years. There are usually more women than men in the group, which consists on average of twenty members. Participants represent diverse cultures, educational needs and interests and come from countries of Africa, Asia, Latin America and western Europe. Disciplines represented include health, education and community work. The multisectoral nature of the course presents one of its greatest strengths: a group such as this holds a wealth of knowledge and experience. While many conventional sources of knowledge are called upon, we consider the experience and knowledge participants bring to the course to be of crucial importance and the methodology adopted seeks to give participants' perspectives a central voice.

The two of us who co-ordinate the course have experience in the field of nursing and community health and have both spent a number of years working at community level in Third and First World countries. As course co-ordinators our responsibilities include curriculum development, teaching and tutorial work, assessment and evaluation activities, course promotion, admissions and administration, as well as research development and networking with others pursuing similar educational and social goals. A large proportion of our time is spent in tutorial work, particularly in relation to overseas students, who often have complex problems of funding, accommodation, coping with the stress of racism, and problems of ill health in a strange country with no immediate family support.

As women (tutors) we are seen by some students to be more approachable than male tutors regarding personal issues, in the sense that many cultures see women as the carers, whilst our male colleagues tend to be viewed as academic specialists, but not leant upon in times of personal stress. A major aim of the course, however, is to challenge just such assumptions! Whilst we see the maintenance role aspect of our work as integral to effective education, and can see it is much appreciated by course participants, invariably it occupies a great deal of time and is rarely recognised or valued by the university. An advantage of our gender is that we offer confidence to many women group members. Many have told us they feel a sense of solidarity with us, even though we may have little other than gender oppression in its broadest sense in common.

Critical education and empowerment
We are strongly motivated to work towards critical education in the belief that it is empowering education. We believe that education should involve students in efforts to identify their own problems, to critically analyse the historical, cultural and socio-economic roots of these and to develop strategies to create positive change in their lives and communities. Yet our work towards CE today takes place against a background of change in higher education which is increasingly antagonistic to our goals.

The ethos of the market place has entered universities, with the Government's Charter for Higher Education promoting the concept of students as consumers (DFE, 1993). Consumer rights, value for money and customer satisfaction are the language of consumer empowerment from the new Right perspective. But while such changes may increase the power of central government over universities, reducing their autonomy and making them more accountable, it is questionable how far they genuinely empower students, whose rights are narrowly circumscribed and do not include the right to ask fundamental questions concerning the nature of the education offered them. This consumerist approach highlights the Government's functionalist perspective on education, seeing it primarily as a means of producing a more highly educated workforce capable of competing effectively in world markets and increasing Britain's economic prosperity. Their concept of empowerment rests on a consensus view of society, seeing the role of education as being to enhance the individual's capacity to function effectively within the system and thus to maintain the *status quo* (Jarvis, 1985).

A more radical understanding of empowerment starts with a critique of the distribution of power in society, recognising the historical and structural forces which influence the distribution of power. It sees the formal education system as a means by which existing balances of power are maintained, through the promulgation of establishment knowledge, values and beliefs (Faure 1972). Traditionally, formal education involves the transmission of expert knowledge from teacher to learner.

'Knowledge is handed down . . . like a corpse of information – a dead body of knowledge – not a learning connection to . . . reality' (Shor 1987:4).

Those in power construct and control knowledge and, through the transmission of that knowledge and the values inherent within it, educate people into a state of disempowerment and socialise them into inequality (Freire, 1972; Shor 1992). Clearly, from this perspective, education which is genuinely empowering calls not for commercial consciousness but for critical consciousness. It offers a vision of a more just world and becomes a means of working towards social and political change.

Most empowering approaches to education are found outside the formal education system, in the community context (Wallerstein and Bernstein 1988, Kirkwood 1991). But there is growing recognition that empowerment at a community level calls for changes in professional perspectives and values: that in order to be able to work in an empowering way, professionals need to experience empowerment for themselves, in their own education and professional training (Fahlberg *et al* 1991). Thus there is a strong argument for promoting empowering educational approaches at universities, the education and training grounds of the professions. But how well prepared are we to engage in university education which is genuinely empowering?

Central to the practice of CE is the concept of critical pedagogy: the critical examination of received wisdom and the taken-for-granted beliefs and values that underpin it (Kelly 1986).Though in theory the questioning of received wisdom may sit easily with the notion of higher education, the practice may be flawed in several ways. Firstly, the notion of critical dialogue is closely linked to the use of participatory learning methods. While in higher education, as in education generally, there has been a move away from a didactic to a more participatory approach to teaching it may be argued that, for the most part, control remains firmly with the teachers. A move towards informal, participatory methods may take place without any shift in underlying values. Edwards and Furlong (1985: 24) observed in their research on progressive methods in schools that

' . . . beneath some undoubtedly significant departures from traditional
ways of transmitting knowledge in classrooms lay a continuing assumption
that the pupil's task was to move as rapidly as possible towards the
teacher's framework of meanings' (1985:24)

A further difficulty with the notion of critical dialogue is the underlying assumption that critical dialogue is rational dialogue, in which there is space for all perspectives to be heard. Yet the very notion of rational dialogue arguably gives unequal weight to powerful groups (white, male, middle class, heterosexual) and their values and interests, and in the classroom environment the inequalities and power relations of the wider world may be reproduced. In such situations, the encouragement of critical dialogue may be little more than an intellectual exercise, reinforcing the supremacy of abstract theoretical knowledge and denying other forms of knowing. Thus it falls into the trap of the inaction of critical dialogue, failing to make connection with the 'real' world,or to recognise any implications for action or social change (Ellsworth 1994)

For education to be truly empowering there is a need to focus not only on the content of dialogue, but also on the processes taking place within the learning situation. An empowering approach to education calls for a new relationship among learners themselves, and between teacher and learner. It calls too for a new relationship between the learners and knowledge, from passive acceptance to active and critical construction. Such a change can only take place if the teacher, working in a facilitating model, sees herself as a part of a system of oppression and inequality, and is committed to working alongside students to effect change, in theory and in practice, through critical reflection and action.

Towards critical education on the EPHC course
On the EPHC course we are committed to facilitating empowering experiences of learning, though we recognise that the extent to which this is possible depends on a complex set of factors which include course participants' personal investment in challenging the *status quo*, our own energy levels and the wider context of higher education which relentlessly impacts on us, shaping the direction and quality of our work. We understand CE to be as much about educational process it is about educational content. It is an approach to education that offers information that is relevant to each participant's intellectual development, while at the same time strengthening their sense of confidence and self worth in both their personal and professional lives. Course participants should be able to see that their views, opinions and experiences have significance. Not only can they learn from others, but others may learn from them. This can be particularly affirming for those who experience inequality through gender, race or other forces of oppression (Weiler, 1991). Participants are encouraged to see that they have a right to ask questions about the world in which they live (including the classroom) and how this world is organised and controlled. In these ways some, though not all, learn to examine and challenge their own previously held values and perspectives and also those of others. By doing so they can come to a more critical understanding of themselves and the world.

It would be somewhat arrogant to assume that course participants join us without the capacity to think critically. In some students this capacity may be extensively developed. Others may have a well-developed intellectual critique of inequalities yet there may be little evidence in their behaviour of a commitment to converting this intellectual analysis into action in their daily lives and relationships. In our experience this group frequently represents the dominant social groups mentioned above. At the other extreme, course participants may have experienced educational environments in which they have been powerfully dissuaded from questioning dominant assumptions – thus experiences of CE, while possibly challenging and stimulating, may be threatening and induce strong resistance to change. For a minority this will remain the situation for the duration of the course. Yet again, for others, particularly those who have the most to gain in challenging the status quo, the course offers a strengthening and affirming experience. The following comments come from women, many of whom have undergone educational experiences in the formal system that have not recognised or reflected their life experiences and the forces of oppression they daily struggle with:

'One of the positive things I have learned here is that we learn from each other with trust and respect . . .'

'. . . the course has given me confidence in my own ability. . .'

While the process of CE is guided by a facilitator (otherwise referred to above as tutor) both group members and facilitators are learners. Thus learning becomes a mutual process. A crucial quality of this educational process is dialogue. In relationships of dialogue all participants are seen to possess knowledge and have a right to share this within the group, though, in reality, some occupy considerably more space than others. Knowledge is not seen to be held in the hands of the formal group leader alone nor is it seen to reside among a select group (Fritz 1982). participants are encouraged to see themselves and to relate to each other as subjects of learning, all of whom have a contribution to make and are thus active in the learning process. Learning becomes a holistic experience incorporating not only critical examination of theoretical concepts but also a recognition of feelings and critical reflection on beliefs and experiences. The facilitator's concern, rather than to talk at the group, as might occur in more traditional educational situations, is to listen and pose questions at appropriate times to encourage critical thinking around a particular theme or issue of relevance to the group (Hope & Timmel 1984).

The themes that form the central focus for educational content on the course are frequently complex and may be emotive. They might include for, example, issues of inequality as they relate to gender, sexual orientation or mental health.

122

Participants are rarely, if ever, completely without knowledge or opinion on a theme and each person has different perceptions of it according to their experiences and values. An example of the facilitator stimulating a process of critical reflection in the context of an everyday 'class' might occur when in the midst of a discussion on gender-sensitive research a male member of the group (we shall call him Paul) makes this point:

Paul: 'If I came across 2 books about research methods and one book was written by a man and the other by a woman, I would take the book written by the man.'

Facilitator: 'Why do you say that?'

Paul: 'Because men have a greater capacity to think in a logical and rational way and so their work is of a better intellectual quality than a woman's. . . . '

Facilitator: 'What do others think about what Paul is saying?'

If the group has a number of articulate women within it they are likely to challenge the sexist assumptions that underlie Paul's statement. They may do this from the position of their experiences or by drawing on more-formal sources of knowledge. Some members of the group may be reticent to join in. These the facilitator will try to encourage to take their space in group discussion over a period of weeks and months. Encouraging others to talk as freely as possible, she listens carefully so she can gather information that will provide material for the posing of further questions to stimulate critical inquiry. When discussion of the theme has taken place from a variety of perspectives the facilitator may offer further information to help participants develop a more questioning view of the theme. In our present example, she might pose such questions as:

'Why do some members of the group agree with the way Paul sees the issue while others see things very differently?'

'What are the factors in our upbringing and daily life activities that encourage us to hold the view we hold?'

'Have you always held this view?'

'Who/what helped you to question it?'

'Is it possible to change the way we understand the world to be?'

In facilitating critical dialogue, the facilitator needs to be aware of personal feelings and power struggles in the group and to work to establish a sensitive and aware political and cultural climate for learning. In this way, she helps group members to see themselves as a microcosm of the wider society, to understand that many of the power divisions that exist 'out there', exist also within the group. This can stimulate critical thinking around the way oppressive forces impact on the daily life experiences of group members, and participants may become aware that we all have the potential both to create change and to set up resistance to it, and in so doing to have an impact on the world in which we live.

The above serves to demonstrate something of the problem-posing (Freire 1972) quality of CE as developed on the EPHC course. Dialogue takes place when group members analyse and share perceptions of a theme that is of interest to them and on which they may wish to take action. This participatory and experience-focused approach emerges from our understanding of the process and purpose of CE. The broad aim is for participants themselves to become '. . . theorists of their own lives by analysing their own experiences. . .' (Weiler 1991:462).

Power and conflict in critical education

Clearly, not everyone feels at home with the processes of CE and most of us are unfamiliar with working in this way in a formal education context. Many course participants have told us they find the course a stimulating and challenging educational experience; others initially feel threatened and may seek to detach themselves from the process element; a minority of participants, however, remain resistant to CE throughout the course. Involvement in CE processes is encouraged not only through problem-posing methodology in the classroom, but also by group-focused assessment procedures, developed partly in response to student interest and need but also to encourage more collective ways of learning. Thus one module assessment involves working together in groups, developing critical analysis of issues in both research and group work practice. Passive or individualistic learning is difficult to maintain in this educational context.

Resistance is particularly visible among participants whose status and power are most threatened by CE. This resistance may be shown, for example, through the denial of the value of experiential knowledge and the insistence that traditional academic sources (predominantly representing white, middle class and male views) are the only valid sources of knowledge. Conflict and confusion may emerge when long established values and beliefs that have been the foundation of a student's life are challenged through the course. At such a time students may experience alienation from their roots and an initial confusion or anger at the uncertainty and insecurity they face, while unable to see a clear path to follow in place of what is left behind. At such times their anger may be focused on the facilitator, who needs to be able to support students through these lonely and testing periods, and herself needs the support of colleagues.

Conflict also comes to the fore in the group exercises which are part of the formal assessment procedure. Groups of five or six students carry out research into a theme given to them by the facilitators and after a period of eight weeks present their work in written and oral forms for assessment and a collective grade. This is a complex exercise bringing together people with a range of different experiences, values and beliefs. As group members struggle to make connections across gender, culture, class and race, high levels of anxiety may develop. The more confident students may confront the facilitators, angry at being exposed to this stressful experience. In preparing students for this exercise time is spent discussing difficulties that might occur, examining why these *do* occur and how they might be handled.

A major challenge in working with CE in a formal educational context is well illustrated in the last example. We refer to the contradictions inherent in the dual role of the facilitator as supportive colleague on the one hand and institutional examiner on the other. Such a dual role calls into question the traditional balance of power between lecturers and students in the hierarchically organised institution of the university and may create confusion and tension both for students and facilitators. Whatever changes may be incorporated into the system, academics continue to hold power over students. Yet power and authority should not in themselves be assumed to be negative attributes: together, facilitator and students need to analyse potential sources of power within the group (information, experience, skills as well as status, reward power, etc) and consider how these can be used in creative and constructive ways within a CE context.

The abuse of power must, however, be guarded against. Those in positions of structural power, be they lecturers or students, may be unaware of the ways they abuse power. As women and as facilitators of CE, our experience in challenging male students who abuse their power in the learning situation has been particularly difficult. (Weiler 1991) draws attention to the need for women to claim authority in a society that denies this to them. The expectations that patriarchal societies have of women are that they

> '... are not meant to think analytically about society, to question the way
> things are, to consider how things could be different. Such thinking
> involves an active not a passive, relationship to the world' (Weiler
> 1991:462).

The authority of a woman lecturer is almost inevitably in question from course participants from the start, in a way in which a male lecturer's authority may never be questioned. We have found that it may take many weeks or months successfully to challenge these deeply ingrained values and beliefs. Change may be possible through encouraging open, honest and critical discussion of these issues, allowing space for often deep seated and powerful feelings gradually to be expressed.

Constraints and contradictions
in working towards CE in a university setting

The above discussion makes clear the challenging nature of CE: it demands considerable time and skill. While we remain strongly committed to the values of CE, we find it increasingly difficult to maintain this approach to education in the university environment of today. Instead we find ourselves struggling against a tide of institutional changes that force us towards a more-lecture-focused, non-creative, bureaucratic educational role. Our time is increasingly channelled away from teaching and the skills of teaching are being downgraded.

The major expansion in student numbers in recent years (DFE 1994), unmatched by an accompanying rise in the number of academic teaching staff, has resulted in heavier teaching loads. At the same time, changes in the government system for funding universities has meant increasing pressure on all academic staff to be more research active. In addition, the introduction of quality assessment in teaching and research has led to an increase in the administrative workloads of academic staff, further diminishing the time available for both teaching and research (AUT 1994). With universities under severe financial pressure, lecturers leaving their employment are often not replaced, a growing proportion of academic staff are employed on short term contracts, and teaching-only contracts are under discussion, a move which may potentially further downgrade the status of teaching academics. A major concern in this respect is the growing practice of drawing on postgraduate students (PGS) for teaching purposes. While this may provide benefits for the PGS in developing teaching skills and exploring possibilities of employment opportunities, there remains the danger of exploitation. The PGS may be in a position to contribute appropriate knowledge; she or he may not, however, have the necessary teaching experience and skills to do so effectively and both she or he and the students may be compromised as a result. This raises questions about the recognition afforded to the importance and the skills of teaching.

An academic's time is increasingly monitored in terms of production. Productiveness however, is measured principally as production of research and publications – output designed to increase the university's research ratings – rather than quality of teaching. Research publications have traditionally been the principal criterion for career progression in universities, and efforts to gain fuller recognition for teaching appeared until recently to be gaining ground. Today, however, the establishment of the research assessment exercise as the basis for university funding means that, for the individual academic, failure to achieve a sufficient level of research funding and publications not only reduces the chances of career progression but, increasingly, threatens job security itself. While research activities are important to the quality of academic teaching, this should not be at the expense of face-to-face contact with students. If a lecturer leaves the university it has been our experience that she or he is rarely replaced. Those who are employed on short term contracts steadily grow in number. Under these circumstances, effective planning of long term course development becomes nigh impossible. Today we work in a university system where insecurities abound and morale is often low. Faced with increasing workloads and trying to balance the competing demands of teaching, research and administration, as well as taking account of the needs of our families, our partners and our lives outside the university we find ourselves faced with the question: can we afford to continue our present level of commitment to CE on the EPHC course?

There is less and less time to spend in teaching and tutorial contexts and increasing pressure to move away from group work and participatory methods towards lecturing as the predominant mode of teaching. This has implications for all academics and most certainly for those who are committed to CE. We are not only concerned to work with students in exploring the politics of education and health as academic topics but also to make connections across the personal experiences of students and the wider political and economic contexts from which those experiences emerge. Many of our students come from countries which are facing major economic, social and political upheaval, and they have strong ties and commitments to families, friends and colleagues back home. Tutorials provide us with the opportunity to relate to students in their wider environments and to offer personal as well as academic support at an individual level. How, for example, do we deal with a situation where a student has heard from home that a civil war has broken out in her country and she has no idea of the whereabouts of her family in the midst of widespread violence? Another example might be if an elder in a student's family has died unexpectedly and the student finds himself responsible for the care of his parents yet so far from home? Tutorials provide an opportunity for the tutor to maintain close contact with the student at such times, should the student want this. They have a crucial quality to contribute to CE, yet they are threatened by the growing practice of restricting time allocated for tutorial and supervision activities.

The fact that the course attracts large numbers of overseas students to a UK educational establishment brings yet a further contradiction into play. There are educational benefits to be had from bringing people from many countries together to study within an atmosphere of dialogue. At the same time this also provides substantial income for the university. The question of whether the course should be taking place in the UK as opposed to a Third World country remains. We believe that encouragement and support to students to establish such courses in their own countries and regions of the world are of prime importance. However, if and when they occur it is likely to conflict with the economic interests of the university.

In conclusion, whilst we maintain a firm belief in the value of CE, we are aware that it is becoming increasingly difficult to pursue. The threat to maintaining the educational methodology developed on the EPHC course is very real. The Government's promotion of business relationships and consumer rights, of economic values and output measures, of quantity before quality, is at odds with the humanist approach of our work and creates a conflict in values espoused on the course. We find ourselves working in an increasingly individualistic, competitive environment which runs counter to our beliefs about the nature and purpose of education. The very act of writing this chapter in a collaborative way is part of our struggle to survive, to network, to disseminate and to share our ideas with others who remain committed to this educational philosophy. It is also a way of making visible our struggle which otherwise remains largely unacknowledged within the institution of the university.

References

Association of University Teachers (1994). *Long Hours, Little Thanks*. Survey by the Association of University Teachers. AUT, London.

DFE (1993). *The Charter for Higher Education.*

DFE (1994). Student Numbers in Higher Education – Great Britain 1982/83 to 1992/93. *Statistical Bulletin* 13/94. August.

Doyal, L. (1995). *'What makes women sick?'* Macmillan.

Edwards, A. D. and Furlong, V. J. (1985). Reflections on the Language of Teaching. In: Burgess R. (Ed) (1985) *Field Methods in the Study of Education*. Falmer Press, London.

Ellsworth, E. (1994). 'Why Doesn't This Feel Empowering? Working Through the Repressive Myths of Critical Pedagogy' in *Harvard Educational Review*, Vol 39, No 3: 297-324.

Fahlberg, Larry. L.; Poulin, Amy. L.; Girdano, Daniel. A. and Dusek, Dorothy. E, (1991). Empowerment as an Emerging Approach to Health Education. *Journal of Health Education* 22(3): 185-193.

Faure, Edgar (1972). *Learning to Be: The World of Education Today and Tomorrow.* UNESCO, Paris.

Freire, P. (1972). *Pedagogy of the Oppressed,* Penguin.

Fritz, C. (1982). *Because I Speak Cockney, They Think I'm Stupid: An Application of Paulo Freire's Concepts to Community Work with Women,* Association of Community Workers in the UK, London.

Hope, A. and Timmel, S. (1984). *Training for Transformation,* Mambo Press, Zimbabwe.

Jarvis, Peter (1985). *The Sociology of Adult and Continuing Education.* Croom Helm, Kent.

Kelly, A. V. (1986). *Knowledge and Curriculum Planning.* Harper & Row, London.

Kirkwood, Gerri. (1991). Freire Methodology in Practice. In: *Open University Health Education Unit (1991) Roots & Branches.* Papers from the OU/HEA 1990 Winter School on Community Development and Health. Open University, Milton Keynes.

Mies, M. and Shiva, V. (1993) *'Ecofeminism',* Zed Books.

Mohanty, C. (1991) *'Third World Women and the Politics of Feminism',* Indiana University Press.

Sanders, D. (1985) *'The Struggle with Health',* Macmillan, London.

Shor, I. (Ed.) (1987) *'A Source Book for Liberatory Teaching'* Heinman, Portsmouth, New Hampshire.

Shor, I. (1992). *Empowering Education: Critical Teaching for Social Change: 4,* University of Chicago Press, Chicago.

Wallerstein, Nina and Bernstein, Edward (1988). Empowerment Education: Freire's Ideas Adapted to Health Education. *Health Education Quarterly* 15(4): 379-394.

Weiler, K. (1991) 'A Feminist Pedagogy of Difference'. *Harvard Educational Review,* Vol 61 No.4, November: 449-474.

WHO (1978) *Alma Ata Declaration,* WHO, Geneva.

Chapter 9
Empowerment in Social Work:
The Case of CCETSW's Welsh Language Policy

Elisabeth Lynn and Allan Muir

*no personne or personnes that use the Welsshe speche or langage shall have
or enjoy any maner office or fees within the Realme of Englonde Wales or
other the Kinges dominions upon peyne of forfaiting the same offices or fees
onles he or they use and exercise the speche or langage of Englisshe*

Act of Union 1536

Introduction

Our intention is to discuss the consequences of introducing, into social work
training in Wales, a recognition of the need to acknowledge the Welsh language.
This was done in 1989 through CCETSW's[1] Welsh Language Policy being incorporated into what became known as 'Paper 30' (CCETSW, 1991). Now, six years
later, CCETSW has tried to remove the Welsh Language Policy from its latest
version of Paper 30 (CCETSW, 1995)[2]. Why? To what extent can the response to
this Policy during these six years be understood in terms of empowerment and disempowerment, and how fruitfully has that window of time been used? 'What
lessons are to be learnt and what of the future?

We shall begin by giving a general account of how we shall use the term 'empowerment'. We then situate the Welsh language policy of CCETSW in the history of
Welsh oppression and discuss its role in empowering Welsh social workers and
their clients. Some peculiar features of Wales in relation to the Welsh language are
discussed which introduce complexities and contradictions into the discussion of
empowerment.

An Interpretation of Empowerment

We are aware that the term 'empowerment' is contentious. Rather than try to
address the complex issue of its different meanings, which are well stated in
Dalrymple and Burke (1995), we shall just say how we intend to use it here. We
feel that the various ways in which it is employed derive from something more
fundamental the way in which the social order is seen to be structured so we start
with a few words on how we perceive this structure.

We take it as axiomatic that society is multiply fractured into groups with differ-
ential power[3] positions, by divisions such as race, class, gender, language, etc.
Every such instance of power is also a site of oppression. Individuals are born into

a pre-existent world and come to occupy places on sides of the various divides. Where they are placed partly structures their consciousness and their possibilities for change. Individuals, and the collectives to which they belong, or to which they owe allegiance, are interrelated dialectically; the individual is determined, but not completely so, by her social being and, conversely, no collective is fully reducible to its individual members.

We want to apply the word 'empowerment' to an individual or to a group. One immediate definition which might suggest itself would simply be the acquisition of power as a result of an intended act. However, this is too neutral for our purposes, since we do not wish the acquisition of increased power by an oppressing group to be so labelled; rather, we shall reserve it for the intentional acquisition of power by an oppressed group or individual member(s) thereof. This means that any use of the term will always refer to a particular oppression.

The intention to empower, who is to be empowered and how, is determined, not only by the view of the social order, but by the value base adopted. However, the *methods* of empowerment are the same though not, of course, equally available. Empowerment may be attempted through person-to-person counselling, encouragement, education of an individual, or by policies and legislation designed to strengthen the rights of a group.

In order to develop our model of the relationship between an individual and a group, consider the following complex of possibilities.

1(a) Empowerment of an individual can empower a group to which she belongs;

1(b) Empowerment of a group can empower its members.

2(a) Gaining of power by an individual can detach her from a group;

2(b) Empowerment of a group can diminish the power of a member.

In the way we employ the term, 'empowerment' must be in reference to the enhancement of power of an oppressed group, or of an individual representative of that group. 1(a) and 1(b) form an inseparable dyad in that, by definition, some particular oppression is being addressed and the individual(s) concerned is (are) only to be considered in their role as a member(s) of an oppressed group. (To avoid, henceforth, the clumsy typography of the last sentence, the word 'individual' will be taken to refer to both its singular and plural senses.)

We reject, however, two common interpretations of this interplay between individual and group, which are but two sides of a romantic myth. One employs the language of 'leadership', 'loyalty' and the like, being most familiar from the class politics of Leninist parties; the other proposes a cosy blending between individual and group, forming a basis for *identity* politics discussed critically in Sivanandan (1995). Applied to an oppressor's side of a social division, these are just the major components of Fascist ideology!

Either view, or both, can arise from concentration upon a single oppression. However, because of the multiplicity of groups to which an individual may belong, and the multifarious natures of the individuals within a group, we must recognise the possibility of conflicts between groups and between (even within) individuals. Empowering A might empower or disempower B; acknowledging that possibility is an essential part of any useful debate on empowerment. All activities of empowerment are to be seen within a dynamic framework of inter-relations. So any shift of power inevitably has repercussions beyond its immediate intention and arises from a combination of often conflicting interests, requiring continuous re-evaluation of what has been achieved.

2(a) and 2(b) above point to possible modes of dislocation between an individual and a group; they arise logically from our decision that 'empowerment' shall always refer to some particular oppression. However, they are presented too starkly and should be regarded only as a shorthand reminder of all the complexities spelled out in the previous paragraph. An individual belonging to a number of oppressed groups will make choices of emphasis in commitment of time and energy. It is possible that events strengthening the person in one respect might be seen to diminish their contribution in another. Audre Lorde remarks:

> 'As a Black lesbian feminist comfortable with many different ingredients of my identity, and a woman committed to racial and sexual freedom from oppression, I find I am constantly being encouraged to pluck out some one aspect of myself and present this as the meaningful whole, eclipsing or denying the other parts of myself. But this is a destructive and fragmenting way to live' (Lorde, 1984).

And, of course, most people are still struggling gamely towards that degree of integral self-identity. Other dislocations arise between a group and dissident members who desire change from within.

Certain exaggerations of inevitable differences may occasion doubts about the value of the term 'empowerment'. New Right philosophies emphasise the potential of an individual for independent action, seeing group affiliations as limitations, and will hence frame a concept of empowerment to that end; this is well discussed by Baistow (1994/5). In similar spirit, but with a more truly liberatory purpose, the post-modernist challenge to grand narratives emphasises the indefinite multiplicity of perspectives (Howe, 1994). As bell hooks has insisted, though, this disruption of generalising accounts of reality should not be deployed – or, perhaps, deployed only with extreme caution – against new narratives emerging from oppressed groups, attempting to articulate some commonalities of their experience (hooks, 1991).

Points 1 and 2 help guard against various errors of undue emphasis which we have outlined. It requires fine and specific judgement to decide the relative strengths and potentialities between and within contending claims. The living politics of a particular struggle requires alertness to general trends, but also to nuances of difference within those generalities. 'Whether there will again arise confident generalised theories adequate to account for the variety of oppressions, with useful guidance for combating them, remains for the future to decide. For the moment, the complexity of human experience and all the manifold accounts from differing perspectives must be taken piecemeal.

The demise of confidence in overarching general theories throws doubt upon broad agendas for social research. Instead of positivist investigations within a grand paradigm, we have more tentative modes of inquiry which seek to grasp the full richness of a more limited domain. Here we adopt the case study approach to a specific instance of empowerment.

Empowerment through language?
For the first time in the history of social work education, Paper 30 clearly formulated a set of anti-oppressive values to underpin the training and future practice of social work students. For example, qualifying social workers would be required to

'demonstrate an awareness of both individual and institutional racism and ways to combat both through anti-racist practice' (page 16).

The second edition of Paper 30(1991) contained three important annexes supporting CCETSW's approach, namely:

Annex 5: Statement on Anti-racism;

Annex 6: Equal Opportunities Policy;

Annex 7: Welsh Language Policy.

These were bold, if overdue, statements of intent to complement with values of social justice, the liberal, individualist tradition of social work. So demonstration f these alternative values became a requirement for qualification. They have now een eliminated from the latest revision of Paper 30 (CCETSW, 1995) – see, owever, footnote 2 – and it remains to be seen to what extent future courses will e able to maintain an anti-oppressive component.

)ur concern here is with Annex 7 within which the following three principles are tated:

- CCETSW should promote and encourage equal status for the Welsh and English languages in its work in Wales.

- A client has a basic right to choose the language of interaction with the social work agency.

- CCETSW should seek to ensure that Welsh medium education and training are available for students, and that English medium education and training are culturally and linguistically sensitive.

Iere, within the context of the Welsh language, we find an intention to empower he Welsh-speaking community and the individuals within that community – ervice users and providers as well as students and their teachers. This is not an solated issue; it needs to be understood in the wider context of the history of ppression of the Welsh language and the struggle, in the modern era, to defend nd renew the language.

)ur aim here is only to trace some key events that are relevant to the focus of this hapter. Our starting point is the Act of Union 1536, which was designed

'fully to incorporate Wales as part of England, politically, administratively, linguistically and in the administration of the law' (Davies, 1994, page 42).

The effect of this legislation was to make English the language of officialdom, of he powerful ruling institutions, relegating the Welsh language to the home and to veryday talk of folk, where it was, overwhelmingly, the only language of the najority. The effect of the erosion of the language in official circles and the process of anglicisation of the powerful Welsh aristocracy, resulting in the collapse of centuries-old sponsorship for Welsh poetry and culture, took its toll on he political and linguistic standing of the Welsh language in Wales. How did it urvive at all? Religion and education have played major parts in Welsh history, oth as sustainers and destroyers of the language. In 1588, William Morgan, the vicar of Llanrhaedr ym Mochnant, translated the Bible into Welsh and the signifi-ance of this feat cannot be overestimated. In fact, some people would go so far as to claim that his achievement in producing a work of such quality and poetry saved the language from extinction. Comparisons have been made between the relative strength of the Welsh language today and the position of the Irish and Scots Gaelic languages where there were no such (early) translations. Griffith Jones (1683-1761) rector of Llanddowror is another significant figure in Welsh history. He established schools to teach children and adults the catechism – but doing so in *Welsh*: 3,325 schools were established in 1,600 different locations attended by 250,000 pupils (Davies, 1993, page 29). An amazing accomplishment by any standard! Contrast this grass root activity with the Education Report of 1847 which came to be known as *Brad y Llyfrau Gleision* (Treachery of the Blue Books). It stated:

'The evil of the Welsh language . . . is obviously and fearfully great in the courts of justice . . . it distorts the truth, favours fraud, and abets perjury, which is frequently practised in courts and escapes detection through the loop holes of interpretation. . . . The mockery of an English trial of a Welsh criminal by a Welsh jury addressed by counsel and judge in English is too gross and shocking to need comment. It is nevertheless a mockery which must continue until the people are taught the English language; and that will not be done until there are efficient schools for the purpose' (quoted by Harris, 1991).

Harris continues:

'It is quite apparent that the possession of an independent language was considered a threat by the dominant class and dominant culture in English society' (ibid. page 138).

Eventually the Education Act of 1870, with its linguistically devastating English curriculum and its insistence on the English language, brutally carried out the spirit of the 1536 Act of Union.

It is impossible here to detail the complexity of Welsh history through the Industrial Revolution, the non-conformist religious revivals, the establishment of the university colleges of Aberystwyth (1872), Cardiff (1883), Bangor (1884) etc. We refer the interested reader to the works of the eminent Welsh historian, Ieuan Gwynedd Jones (1981) where she will find many instances of Welsh attempts to resist the English language onslaught. But of course the power of legislation to enforce the English language proved to be wellnigh overwhelming. It was in 1938, following the celebrated trial at Caernarfon of Saunders Lewis,

Lewis Valentine and D. J. Williams for setting fire to a bombing school at Llŷn, where the judge refused their demand to address the court in Welsh, that a movement was launched at the National Eisteddfod to repeal the language clause of the Act of Union and call for the Welsh language to have equal validity with English in Wales. It was the same Saunders Lewis (noted academic, dramatist and political activist) who, in his dramatic radio lecture of 1962, Tynged yr Iaith Gymraeg (Fate of the Welsh Language), predicted the death of the language unless action was taken to reverse the effects of the four-hundred-year-old oppression. He urged listeners to

> '. . . make it impossible to conduct local authority or central government business in Wales without the Welsh language' (from Davies, 1993).

The timing and strength of his pronouncements not only caught the imagination of Welsh speakers but prompted a will to act. In 1963 *Cymdeithas yr Iaith Gymraeg* (Welsh Language Society) was founded and has campaigned consistently on the basic principle that people in Wales have the right

> to use their own language in courts, in communication with official bodies, in education, etc. To deny that right is an oppression.

Note that here is an excellent illustration of how an individual, within a context of oppression, used an opportunity to empower a group. This resulted in the burgeoning of a broader based movement fighting for Welsh language rights on several fronts. There was a successful campaign for a Welsh television channel; there was a growth of Welsh medium education across the continuum from nursery schools to university, and an increasing number of public bodies adopted bilingual policies – for example Gwynedd County Council on its establishment in 1974. None of this would have been possible without the passing of three pivotal Acts of Parliament – the Welsh Courts Act 1942, Welsh Language Act 1967 and the Welsh Language Act 1993 – with Parliament finally accepting that Welsh should have equal validity with English in the administration of law and public services in Wales. The Act of 1993, although subject to criticism Davies, (1993), also established a statutory Welsh Language Board to promote and facilitate the use of Welsh. Public bodies are now required to prepare language schemes setting out the services which they provide through the Welsh language.

Where does social work fit in?

The British Association of Social Workers (BASW) agreed to support a bilingual policy as far back as 1979, and in 1984 produced a declaration on the use of Welsh and English in social work practice in Wales. One of their main arguments was based on the notion of 'good practice', centred on the belief that social workers should start where the client is at. In Wales, this meant being prepared to use the Welsh language. This position was accepted and strengthened by CCETSW in their Welsh Language Policy published in 1989 where they state the client's right to expect a service in Welsh. The Policy was the result of CCETSW's Committee in Wales setting up a subgroup in 1987 to develop a Welsh Language Policy and appointing its first Welsh-speaking staff member to assist the work. The membership of the committee consisted of key people involved in social work practice and education in Wales and although they came from a variety of backgrounds (and probably had a variety of aims in working for a Welsh Language Policy) they produced a framework for action based on three principles (which form the text of Annex 7 above) which have been substantially, but not fully, implemented at the time of writing. Williams (1994) remarks that the main deficiency is in implementation of the third principle. He notes that:

> 'Constant dissatisfaction has been expressed by students on qualifying courses about the comparative lack of all kinds of learning opportunities through the medium of Welsh. Their observations are summed up memorably in the statement that Welsh appears to be a problem for courses rather than an opportunity to improve and enhance the teaching.'

His observation prompts the question – what has to happen to turn 'the problem' into a positive force? What are the necessary conditions for empowerment?

Embedding the Welsh Language Policy within Paper 30 was a clear indication of CCETSW's intention that its contents were to be included in the new DipSW (Diploma in Social Work) programmes, and there is evidence that programmes throughout Wales are tackling the issue, that is, using the policy to empower students. In the predominantly English-speaking South Wales Programme a bilingual handbook has been produced, a Welsh-speaking member of staff has been appointed and they are piloting Welsh medium modules. In the North and West Wales Consortium where, in one site, two-thirds of the course is Welsh-speaking, the policy has been implemented so that Welsh-speaking students now have Welsh-speaking tutors, practice teachers, Welsh written assignments marked in Welsh (although a minority still have to be translated, translation checked by the student), bilingual documentation, and a pilot Welsh medium module. Two additional major developments are in the pipeline:

- a Welsh Charter for students
- the implementation of a Welsh medium DipSW route on the basis of the recommendations of a feasibility study carried out in 1994 on behalf of the Consortium.

In summary, the Welsh Language Policy has demonstrably empowered Welsh-speaking students – as well as their lecturers and practice teachers – and the empowerment of students and educators is unequivocally linked to the empowerment of users.

But oppressive practice does not automatically disappear with a language policy. As Beatrix Campbell reminded the audience at a day conference (on Anti-Discriminatory Practice in Social Work, 4 May 1995), it is essential to guard against complacency, falling into the trap that paper agreements are synonymous with *actual* achievement. Gains have been made and deserve acknowledgement, but it is naïve – and dangerous – to rest on laurels in the belief that the fight has been won. The implementation of policies has to be constantly evaluated to monitor agreements and incorporate new objectives resulting from changes.

CCETSW is clear on why a policy is necessary – the client's right to choose the language of interaction with the social work agency; it follows then that the touch-stone of whether the policy is succeeding or not is the extent to which Welsh-speaking clients are able to speak Welsh with agencies. There is still work to be done here. For instance, within the recent experience of one of the authors, an eighty-year-old woman, whose first language is Welsh, was to be discharged from hospital to a nursing home, probably on a permanent basis. Not surprisingly she was anxious in the face of such a major emotional and practical upheaval. The social worker who visited her on the ward spoke only English, so the elderly woman was unable to communicate her wishes and fears about the future in the language of her choice – in spite of CCETSW's Welsh Language Policy!

> 'Social work encounters are often stressful affairs, dealing with individuals
> in crisis or discussing private and emotional concerns. How much more
> acute do these difficulties become when the person facing such predica-
> ments is also obliged to force such thoughts and feelings through a language
> which is itself a barrier to effective communication' (Drakeford, 1993).

Old people, young children, people with learning difficulties, anybody under stress and seeking help, are not making a political statement or big cultural debating point when speaking Welsh; they just open their mouths and Welsh comes out. The oft-stated question 'they speak English, don't they'?' is offensive in such situations. In any interaction which touches on our deep sense of self, all of us need to use our preferred language.

Language and Empowerment - and Race
We have outlined a simple oppressor/oppressed situation above. But real life is more complicated! We have described and discussed a case of mutual empow-erment between individual and group which falls under headings 1(a) and 1(b).

We now turn to some issues under 2(a) and 2(b) concerning the complications, interactions and tensions one expects to find in any process of change. When the energy is up and running everyone can benefit, but when doors begin to close there can be a divisive scramble over who will be inside and who outside. What then happens to empowerment?

Any language (Bengali, Welsh, Catalan) bonds an individual to her group; in the act of acquiring a group's language she becomes an automatic exemplar of that group's culture. Were we to discuss empowerment only with regard to Welsh language and the speakers of Welsh, the story would be one of harmonious struggle against external oppression, with a unity of purpose forged by commonality of language – a prime example, in fact, of the romantic search for identity.

But as noted in the first section, a full account of an empowerment should avoid artificial closures and consider also what we summarised above under the headings 2(a) and (b), namely aspects of the whole which are disruptive of simple schemes of closure. The very concept of Welshness exhibits features of intriguing complexity. The majority of Welsh people do not speak Welsh[4] – and the majority of those who do also speak English fluently. It has required an effort of political understanding and will, on the part of the non-Welsh author, to situate the raw facts in their historical context; only then could the apparently disproportionate capacity of the language to empower a Welsh identity be appreciated.

The direct English intention totally to destroy the Welsh language, which we outlined earlier, an intention most perniciously and brutally targeted on children through the education system (Davies 1993) was compounded by massive immigration of workers from England, Scotland, Ireland and elsewhere into burgeoning industrial areas. Paradoxically, this latter event, while helping proportionally to reduce the number of Welsh-language users, created only another strong form of Welsh identity

> ' . . . though it was certainly an experience of uprooting, exile and then integration into a new society, taking three generations to complete, yet its end-product was not assimilation into the culture of the new host, England in this case, but a wholly new and very consciously Welsh community operating with seeming indifference in both English and Welsh' (Conran, 1994-5).

Moreover, Wales did not suffer to the same extent the massive efflux of population such as devastated the economies and cultures of Scotland and Ireland (Davies, 1992).

In the event, even non-Welsh-speakers can have a staunch pride in and respect for the language in its current renaissance. The Welsh Language Acts, particularly their emphasis on education through the medium of Welsh, should strengthen the language in future generations. In fact, the language cannot stabilise in its present minority state; it can only decline effectively to nothing or, responding to the modern world, grow in strength. Everybody knows that the former would be a final, dismal defeat in a ruthless cultural war.

While one must adopt an open-eyed realism about contradictions internal to Wales, these should be considered against a background of the more powerful, historically determining presence of England. Dialectical relations between internal and external aspects of any community give rise to some of the most slippery issues of political analysis. Internal differences must be addressed but, as Lorde has suggested in the quote above, to do this in a fragmenting way is to put a weapon in the arsenal of an external oppressor. Quantitative considerations are frequently deployed, usually coupled to economic accounting, to show that minorities cannot be granted their rights. But rights are not derived from numerical considerations – as is well understood in the context of anti-racism. Precisely because we all belong to many social groups, we all belong to minorities of one sort or another! Head-counting considerations of the language, precisely because they conceptually dismember Wales, support the oppressive role of England; demographic considerations of the class composition of three groups of people living in Wales – Welsh speakers, Anglo-Welsh and Non-Welsh-speaking immigrants – show how this continues to the present day (Aitchison, 1994).

Even this is not the whole story; there are many layers to an onion! Anguishing about the existence of two, often conflicting, modes of Welshness and their relationship to newly influxing English settlement may create a satisfying sense of grasping the rich tapestry of Welsh culture, but if our image is only that of inter-flowing, interacting white people we compound the oppression of Wales's substantial Black population (Williams, 1995). The struggle for the soul of Wales, through struggle around its language, will be weakened if it is not linked actively to struggles against other oppressions within Wales.

Indeed, it is important to understand how the anti-racist policy of CCETSW functioned within the empowerment of the Welsh language. It seems appropriate to single out race from the range of divisions as an anti-racist statement was included (Annex 5) in Paper 30 and CCETSW led its anti-oppressive position through an anti-racist perspective. In the 1980s an anti-racist movement (spearheaded by the Mickleton group) campaigned successfully for a change of policy and approach to race issues within the structures and procedures of CCETSW, culminating in the setting up of the Black Perspectives Committee in 1987. . . .

> 'to assist the Council and its staff to develop effective anti-racist strategies in social work education and training, and encourage the development of CCETSW as a racially sensitive and culturally aware organisation'
> (Council Meeting 10/4/87).

Black representation on CCETSW committees (including the Welsh committee) became a necessity and Welsh language campaigners within CCETSW saw this move as an opportunity also to press their case for an agreement for a formalised Welsh language presence on the CCETSW Cymru/Wales committee. It was an instance of cross-group empowerment – the momentum and gains of one group empowering another[5]

Unfortunately, this is not the end of the story. Following the Press and Government attack on CCETSW's anti-racist policies in the summer of 1993, the appointment of a new chair to get the CCETSW house in order and the edict from central government for a review of training, we now have a revised Paper 30 (CCETSW, 1995) with a weakened Equal Opportunities statement, and no longer containing the annexes on anti-racism and the Welsh language (see Footnote 2). The Black Perspectives Committee has been dismantled. For Welsh language activists and supporters now to become inward looking and campaign on the single language issue would be stultifying, non-productive and a betrayal. It would also miss an opportunity for creating new ways of working within the hitherto untested, but no doubt difficult, areas of language/race and language/class etc. perspectives. These are difficult relationships and the body of knowledge to point the way forward is scant. Wales, however, is uniquely placed to pioneer this approach and social work education in Wales cannot afford to ignore the challenge of empowerment practice which addresses connecting oppressions.

Notes
[1] The Central Council for Education and Training in Social Work – the national body for validating social work courses at every level.

[2] At the time of writing (July 1995) things seem to be in flux. The Working Copy, to which Programmes are being asked to submit their DipSW course proposals, does not contain the Policy, and moreover, it is declared that 'the final published version will incorporate final editing only'. There are indications, however, that, following protests, the Welsh Language Policy might be reinstated.

[3] A deep scrutiny of the word 'power' is unnecessary for our purposes. The following will suffice:

'The power of an individual or institution is the ability to achieve something, whether by right or by control or influence. Power is the ability to mobilize economic, social or political forces in order to achieve a result' (Blackburn, 1994)

* According to the Census of 1991, 510,920 inhabitants of Wales (18.7% of the population over the age of three) had some knowledge of Welsh.

* Actually these are instances of self-empowerment. This evokes images of people raising themselves by their own shoelaces, the apparent impossible of which derives from thinking about power via an energy metaphor. As our account of the relationship between Black and Welsh struggles within CCETSW indicates, it is more correctly seen in informational terms. Thus, group A is observed to act forcibly by group B which thereby realises a potential for similar action. Since A has no intention in regard to B, being merely an occasional trigger for B, it cannot be said to empower B, but it is certainly a cause of B's self empowerment.

References

Aitchison, J. and Carter, H. (1994) *Language and class in Wales* Planet, 105, 11-16.

Baistow, K. (1994/5) Liberation and regulation? Some paradoxes of empowerment, *Critical Social Policy*, 42:3, 34~6.

Blackburn, S. (1994) *The Oxford Dictionary of Philosophy*, OUP.

CCETSW (1991/1995) *Rules and Requirements for Education and Training in Social Work 2nd edition/Revised edition)*, CCETSW, London.

Conran, T. (1994-5) *'Anglo-Welsh' Revisited*, Planet 108, 28-34.

Dalrymple, J. and Burke, B. (1995) *Anti-Oppressive Practice, Social Care and the Law*, Open University Press.

Davies, E. (1994) *They All Speak English Anyway*, CCETSW, London.

Davies, G. P. (1994) The Welsh Language and Legislation, in Williams, R. H.; Williams, H. and Davies, E. (eds) *Social Work and the Welsh Language*, CCETSW and University of Wales.

Davies, J. (1992) *Wales and Ireland*, Planet, 95, 7-16.

Davies, J. (1993) *The Welsh Language*. University of Wales Press.

Drakeford, M. (1993) Speaking of Anti-Discrimination, *Probation Journal*, 40:2,78-81.

Harris, V. (1991) Values of Social Work in the Context of British Society in Conflict with Anti-racism, in *Setting the Context for change*, CCETSW.

hooks, b. (1991) 'postmodern Blackness', in *Yearning*, Turnaround.

Howe, D. (1994) Modernity, Postmodernity and Social Work, *British Journal of Social Work*, 24:5,513-531.

Jones, I. G. (1981) *Explorations and Explanations*, Gwasg Gomer.

Lorde, A. (1984) *Sister Outside*,; The Crossing Press.

Sivanandan, A. (interview) (1995) Fighting our fundamentalisms, *Race and Class*, 36:3, 73-81.

Williams, C. (1995) *Race and racism, some reflections on the Welsh context*, Contemporary Wales 8, 113-131.

Williams, H. (1994) Social Work and the Welsh Language, in Williams, R. H.; Williams, H. and Davies, F. (eds) *Social Work and the Welsh Language*, CCETSW and University of Wales.

Subject index

Economic, economy	36
education, adult education, higher education	77, 99, 117
elders, elderly	56, 127
emancipation	36, 58
employment, unemployment	85
empowerment, disempowerment	6, 19, 23, 40, 54, 62, 69, 92, 99, 119, 131
Enlightenment (the)	36
enquiry action learning	113
epistemologies	47, 110
equal opportunities	2, 13, 134
equality, inequality essentialism,	4, 117
essentialist	18, 42
experience, experiential learning	117
exploitation	126
Facilitator	122
family	36, 56
Fascism	8, 95
feminism, feminist, anti-feminist	12, 20, 43, 55, 57, 117
functionalist	119
fundamentalist	7
Gay	18, 29, 45
gaze	106
gender	56, 117
general household survey	56
global	10, 85
grand narratives	59
Health, health promotion,	71, 77, 89, 117
healthy lifestyles, primary health care	13
hegemonic, hegemony	104
hermeneutics	21
heterosexual, heterosexuality	106
hierarchy	8
Hindu	
HIV/AIDS	29, 41
homogeny, homogeneous	59, 107
homophobia	4
homosexual, homosexuality	19
humanism, humanist	113, 128
Identities, identity, identity politics	23, 37, 140
ideology, ideological	89, 101
illness	35, 47
implement, implementation	79
income	86
incorporation	13, 29
India, Indian	8, 78
individual, individualism, individualistic	72, 99
industrialised	85
initiate, initiation	71
injustice	93
isomorphism	109
Knowledge, subjugated knowledge	12, 37, 73, 109, 119